TORONTO

CONSIDERING SELF-GOVERNMENT

Toronto

CONSIDERING SELF-GOVERNMENT

Jane Jacobs, Joe Berridge, Alan Broadbent,
David Crombie, Meric S. Gertler, Richard Gilbert,
Michael Mendelson, David M. Nowlan,
John Sewell, and Enid Slack

Edited by
Mary W. Rowe

The Ginger Press

Design by Lori Ledingham

Canadian Cataloguing in Publication Data

Main entry under title:

Toronto : considering self-government

ISBN 0-921773-50-1

1. Municipal home rule – Ontario – Toronto. 2. Toronto (Ont.) – Politics and government. I. Jacobs, Jane, 1916- . II. Rowe, Mary W., 1959- .

JS1789.3.A3T67 2000 320.8'5'09713541 C00-930112-7

The chapter by Joe Berridge entitled "There's No Need to Sit and Wait for a Handout" has been adapted from *Reinvesting in Toronto: What the Competition is Doing*, published by the Canadian Urban Institute.

Published by
The Ginger Press, Inc.
848 Second Avenue East
Owen Sound, Ontario
Canada N4K 2H3

In conjunction with
ideas THAT MATTER™
a quarterly to stimulate public discourse

Printed in Canada.

Dedicated to
Colin Vaughan (1931 - 2000)
whose steady cajoling for over twenty-five years
helped us recognize the intrinsic status
of Toronto

Contents

Introduction

by Jane Jacobs and Mary W. Rowe

In June of 1999, Alan Broadbent, a private businessman and philanthropist with a long-time interest in all things urban, convened a two-day meeting entitled The Evolution of Toronto, to discuss other forms of governance for the city. The invitation list was modest, limited largely by the logistics of facilitating useful discussions. The attendance list was not representative of the diversity of interest, ethnicity, class and circumstance of Torontonians, but the members recognized their representative weaknesses and, whenever one forgot, another would pointedly remind them.

Nor was the group representative of the many other interests that share a stake in the fate of Toronto, as they extend beyond Toronto, beyond the Greater Toronto Area, beyond the Golden Horseshoe, beyond southern Ontario, beyond central Canada; in fact, they extend across the country and into the northeastern part of the United States, and perhaps even further into the American heartland.

Despite its limitations,* the group was able to raise pertinent questions and provide considerable expertise and experience concerning

* The group included three former mayors, several former municipal councillors, and various academics, activists, journalists and community leaders, plus individuals from varied businesses.

a topic of shared interest and concern: the evolution of Toronto. This volume recounts some of their ruminations, with the objective of sparking consideration of governance among Toronto's widespread constituency. There is nothing definitive here; this book poses questions rather than prescribes answers. It is intended to suggest new avenues of thinking rather than set forth a proposed course of action.

Toronto has become a region of global significance. How we actually define that region geographically may not matter for now; the southern boundary seems to be the only one that is irrefutable. The Toronto region generates wealth, incubates culture, fosters innovation, harbours capital, educates and trains people, welcomes thousands, employs hundreds of thousands, and transports millions every year. Toronto matters – not just to those who live or work in it. It matters to everyone concerned with the economic and cultural vitality of Canada and North America.

Thus, *Toronto: Considering Self-government* is a collection of ideas exploring the conditions that suggest a new form of governance may now be required for the city. Its chapters are derived primarily from papers prepared by their authors as background to the June 1999 meetings – the Mirvish meetings, as they have become affectionately nicknamed, because they took place in one of Toronto's most venerable institutions: The Royal Alexandra Theatre, owned by the Mirvish family. A few chapters were added subsequently including an essay originally published in 1978 by David Nowlan. This book also includes excerpts from discussions that took place during the Mirvish meetings and subsequent smaller group discussions convened through the summer of 1999; these are placed throughout the text as highlights.*

Is self-government for Toronto an idea whose time, finally, has come?

Alan Broadbent argues the infrastructure needs of Toronto go unanswered by senior levels of government with "less specific knowledge, experience or motivation." He surmises that altering the constitutional make-up of Canada to allow for more autonomous cities may be resisted by the federal government – whose singular focus has been

* With the exception of the Nowlan piece, which is presented as it was originally published.

appeasing Quebec – and also by provincial leaders unwilling to cede power. But are those obstacles insurmountable? Is there no opportunity for a "win-win" solution – where a stronger Toronto benefits all?

Broadbent posed three critical questions as precursors to considering self-government: Do the conditions exist for Toronto to assume greater control of its own destiny? What are the potential models for Toronto to do this? What are the political paths to a new governance structure for Toronto?

These three questions formed the basis for the Mirvish meetings and subsequent discussions. The views expressed in this book are varied and there remains plenty of room for dissent and disagreement. Certainly the authors themselves and the participants in these meetings would not necessarily agree on a singular diagnosis of the problem, let alone a preferred solution. And the debate is far from over. Participants continue to have varying views about what is empirically desirable versus what is politically practical. Is independent city-regional government within Canada even thinkable? Would a more Toronto-friendly provincial government make these discussions unnecessary? To the last question, the consensus so far is no. These problems are generally systemic and have little to do with the disposition of a particular elected government. Although one hopes a different provincial government's behavior would be less flagrantly hostile toward its own capital.

> *Essentially, the argument is this: Toronto needs some increased political and financial autonomy to enable it to be an international presence so that it can help Ontario and Canada.*
>
> *Richard Gwyn*

David Crombie traces his sixty-or-so years of association with Toronto and provides a context for the consideration of alternative governance models.

He suggests that Toronto is marked by a vigorous history of citizen engagement, where its denizens have actively worked to prevent harmful development (the Spadina Expressway) and to encourage remediation (Bring Back the Don). Crombie posits that Toronto has been "metropolitanising" for over forty years, but he stops short of suggesting that any change in governance is either desirable or feasible. He suggests that "there are tens of thousands of people who are unconcerned with the nature of relationships between governments, but who care deeply about the issues that are before them."

The next two authors provide contrasting arguments for what one might call the Toronto imperative: get more autonomy or else. Joe Berridge makes a strong case that capital investment in Toronto's aging infrastructure has fallen drastically behind what is required, not only to maintain services at their current level but, more critically, to ensure Toronto is equipped to compete globally. He offers several funding models involving the public and private sectors as means of finding the necessary capital outlays. Berridge does not address the other costs of receiving this type of money – how the giver might perceive the money as some sort of urban largesse. The absence of any exploration of such possible implications in a Canadian context is owing to the fact that his contribution is an abridgment from a research piece his firm produced for the Canadian Urban Institute, entitled *Reinvesting in Toronto: What the Competition is Doing*, which specifically focussed on American examples.

Richard Gilbert was initially asked to prepare a document on what the political paths might be for self-government for Toronto. He deferred, once he'd reviewed the overall meeting agenda, opting instead to lay out a direct appeal for Toronto to assume greater control over decisions of significant environmental importance. Gilbert supports concerns raised by other contributors regarding sprawl; the impact of increased automobile use on global warming is a threat he sees as having an inevitable impact on Toronto. In contrast to Joe Berridge, Gilbert queries the advisability of expanding the airport or creating a superhighway to Buffalo, and suggests that the city needs to find ways soon to diminish our dependency on the job-generating automotive sector.

Meric Gertler examines the economic pillars he sees as critical to determining if the economic conditions present in Toronto support more autonomy. Gertler laments the loss of local control over education spending and taxation and the imposition by the province of a "one size fits all" policy that ignores local requirements. Gertler argues that all of Toronto's economic ducks are pretty much in a row although his principal concern is the absence of a regional "unity of purpose" which he concludes may be "our most scarce commodity."

Gertler's final assertion resonated throughout the Mirvish meetings, where considerable time was consumed discussing the 416-905 area code debate. (Even our usually silent transcriber complained about what she interpreted as "whining.") This led to Michael Valpy suggesting a unified identity be formed for the region, which could be dubbed the 660. ("Area 660: Th°e real Toronto and its real needs for the future," *The Globe and Mail*, Saturday, June 26, 1999)

Is there that significant a gulf between the needs and values of people who live (often not by choice) in the areas outlying the Toronto core and those who live downtown? Does the absence of street cafés in Milton imply those who live there have radically different values to those who frequent Queen Street? And if so, do those value differences prevent the formation of a "unity of purpose" based on the vitality and health of Toronto? Some of the Mirvish participants suggested that one didn't have to live in the core to share urban beliefs such as acceptance of high density or the importance of transit. In fact, they argued, many who find themselves living in the outlying areas would love to live right downtown, but the housing options don't suit them or their jobs are not accessible by transit from downtown.

Enid Slack paints a less-than-optimistic picture of Toronto's current financial ability to pay its own way, given the current rules for municipal finance and revenues. Slack does not query the city's ability to generate wealth. In her view, capturing a share for municipal public needs is what poses the problem. Together with Gertler, Slack provides a kind of reality check. She queries the rationale for downloading social services – a means of income re-distribution – to municipalities that have only property tax from which to finance them. Slack suggests that the combination of cities' inability to share in urban-generated tax revenues (from fuel, sales or income), and their own reluctance to apply user fees for key services (such as garbage disposal or water) hamstrings municipal self-financing. The absence of resources to invest in capital costs of facilities, the increasing costs of sprawl, and the lack of region-wide efforts to establish consistent policies regarding municipal finance, housing, transportation, and land use led Slack to conclude that policy and municipal leadership are not in sync with the economic reality of this global region.

John Sewell raises the most plaintive question: are the values of social justice and cultural vibrancy prized in the portions of the city built before 1950 at odds with the values of individual autonomy and less government presence that infuse portions planned later? He wonders to what extent these values have been reinforced by urban form, pointing out that the greater density of the older portions supported participation and neighbourhood involvement. Sewell questions how the city can begin to think about greater autonomy when common values cannot be assumed and efforts towards enhancing local autonomy will likely be thwarted by "the evil uncle."

Michael Mendelson was invited to explore the political paths and proposes three options: lobby the provincial and the federal governments for more autonomy; create a new, regional level of government; or create an Urban Party and run candidates both provincially and federally.

David Nowlan wrote the final essay twenty years ago. We've included it not only as a tribute to Nowlan for his acute foreknowledge, but also as a reminder of the timelessness of the issue he suggested: "to aim for more legislatively liberated cities." Nowlan's conclusion supports a belief I (Jane Jacobs) first published over thirty years ago: that cities endure – they outlast everything except the carbon that inhabits them – and that facilitating their continued evolution socially, economically and politically is a perpetual task, inherently both necessary and creative.

Toronto is a region and should not be confined by an artificial boundary drawn more than a century ago. Whether people live in Swansea or Buttonville, Erindale or Dunbarton, the point at which their lives converge with others is the new Toronto.

As these authors suggest, this isn't just about economics, although the arguments illustrating that Toronto is an economic region are most compelling. It's about environmental stewardship, social equity, education, housing, the arts. It's also about petty politics, inability to share power, legally entrenched authority versus eyes-on-the street knowledge, delivery of services and redistribution of wealth.

So this inquiry comes as an exploration – a starting point – into some form of self-government for the Toronto region. It speaks to "that deadly interplay" (Jane Jacobs, *Cities and the Wealth of Nations*, Random House, 1984) that develops between nations and their cities as each tries to milk and manipulate the other with the result that both are put into confusion and peril. In fact, this political evolution is proposed as a common sense and practical solution to ensure the ongoing health and vibrancy of the region's economy and life, which would benefit the rest of Canada and its other urban and rural regions.

There are many questions this volume does not address: What would self-government for Toronto look like? Would greater autonomy result in a better – more economically competitive and socially just – Toronto? Subsequent discussions should begin to tackle some of these issues.

In Canada, cities were initially totally dependent, minor subsidiaries of the province but, as the authors of this volume suggest, their development can no longer be constrained by the tutelage of the past. As history has shown us again and again, prospering cities have identities and lifespans of their own. They are not only a country's economic engines, they are places where everything comes together and then is disseminated, again and again and again. And they – like most children – will certainly outlive the circumstances of their parents. To shed old dependencies in order to take on increased responsibilities and more self-reliance is not a sign of failure of either parents or children. Rather, it is the most vital sign of success on the part of both parties, an aim that merits the most serious encouragement and respect.

Jane Jacobs and Mary W. Rowe
Toronto and Owen Sound
January 2000

The Evolution of Toronto

Participants

Max Allen, Producer, Ideas, CBC Radio 1
Carl Amrhein, Dean, Faculty of Arts and Sciences, University of Toronto
Max Beck, Consultant
Morton Beiser, Psychiatrist, Clarke Institute of Psychiatry
Joe Berridge, Partner, Urban Strategies Inc.
Alan Broadbent, Chairman and CEO, Avana Capital Corporation
David Crane, Columnist, *The Toronto Star*
John Crispo, Professor Emeritus, University of Toronto
David Crombie, Chair, Waterfront Regeneration Trust
Ursula Franklin, Professor Emerita, University of Toronto
Greg Gatenby, Artistic Director, Literary Department, Harbourfront Centre
Meric S. Gertler, Professor, University of Toronto
Nathan Gilbert, Executive Director, The Laidlaw Foundation
Richard Gilbert, Consultant
Anne Golden, President, United Way of Greater Toronto
Ken Greenberg, Partner, Urban Strategies
Richard Gwyn, Columnist, *The Toronto Star*
Barbara Hall, Chair, National Strategy on Community Safety and Crime Prevention
J. David Hulchanski, Professor, University of Toronto

Jane Jacobs, Author
Ken Jones, Director, Centre for the Study of Commercial Activity, Ryerson University
Alice Klein, Executive Editor and CEO, *NOW Magazine*
James Knight, Executive Director, Federation of Canadian Municipalities
Dan McAlister, Chairman, Bregman & Hamann Architects
Patricia McCarney, Professor, University of Toronto
James McKellar, Professor, York University
Michael Mendelson, Senior Scholar, The Caledon Institute of Social Policy
Arnold Minors, Consultant
David Peters, General Manager, Ontario Housing Corporation
Richard Rooney, President, Burgundy Assets Management
Mary W. Rowe, Facilitator
John Sewell, Consultant, and Columnist, *eye weekly*
Larry Sherman, Associate, IBI Group
Enid Slack, President, Enid Slack Consulting Inc.
Donald Stevenson, Consultant
Sherri Torjman, Vice President, The Caledon Institute of Social Policy
Michael Valpy, Columnist, *The Globe and Mail*
Colin Vaughan, Broadcaster and Columnist, *The Toronto Star*
David Walsh, Chair, King Bay Chaplaincy
Rodney White, Professor, University of Toronto
Toni Williams, Professor, York University

Cities are the open-ended types of economies in which our open-ended capacities for economic creation are not only able to establish "new little things" but also to inject them into everyday life. Unfortunately, given the deadly interplay between nations and their cities, we human beings are doomed to spurts of economic development only – sporadic and relatively brief episodes, now here, now there, followed by stagnation and deterioration. This must continue unless and until we drift into means of overcoming that deadly interplay itself.

Jane Jacobs, *Cities and the Wealth of Nations*

The Autonomy of Cities in Canada

Alan Broadbent

Canadian cities are creatures of the provinces. The amount of power and authority granted to them by the provinces, whether ample or not, is beyond their control. The provinces have the ability to dissolve municipalities and dismiss their governing councils. The provinces have the ability to dictate the size and structure of city governments, to set the conditions of their ability to raise capital, and to apply duties and obligations to them. The cities have no independent constitutional ability to resist whatever conditions the provinces opt to create for them.

This situation is problematic for cities in Canada, one of the most highly urbanized countries in the world. Its cities, particularly the large cities of Toronto, Montreal, and Vancouver, are the economic, social, and cultural engines of the entire country. Within these urban regions are contained the principal forces which make Canada an effective and competitive modern nation. Yet the cities have very little control over their destinies. They have limited ability to leverage their assets and to maximize their potential. This paper looks at how the areas of infrastructure, politics, and finance relate to this issue.

Infrastructure

Toronto's Pearson Airport is not adequate to serve its economy. Any person engaged in extra-regional business will attest to this. Its capacity is too small, its facilities too limited, and its processes too difficult. There are inadequate transportation links to the airport, the principal lack being a fast rail link connecting it to downtown Toronto and other regions relying on its services.

The redevelopment of Toronto's waterfront continues at a snail's pace. In the 1970s, during a federal election campaign, money was promised to reclaim the waterfront from its industrial and shipping past and make it a vibrant part of the city. Once the original money was spent, little else came from the federal government. The rail corridor which has languished for lack of funds and agreements, maintains a formidable barrier between the city and the lake leaving the Harbourfront neighbourhood cut off from the rest of the city. The other part of the barrier to the lake that remains is the Gardiner Expressway, which is overloaded, expensive to maintain, and ugly, but for which no senior government funds have been allocated for its removal and replacement.

The recent downloading of responsibility for roads from the province to the city, without attendant funds for their upkeep, is the beginning of another cycle of decline for a key piece of infrastructure. The intention of the province to permit extensive development in rural Queensville and allow that area's sewage needs to be added to the Toronto infrastructure, without attendant funds for expansion, further stresses an already stressed utility. And the ongoing delays in approvals for storm sewer holding tank construction further limits the city's ability to deal with its problems effectively and exacerbates degradation of lake water quality.

Continuing provincial reluctance to fund expansion of the urban transit system, coupled with the ongoing encouragement of sprawl development and its required roadways, contributes to worsening air quality in the city and to more traffic congestion in the suburbs. Ongoing federal inflexibility over the expenditure of settlement money for the refugees the federal government admits puts stress on Toronto, and other major cities to a lesser extent, to cope with the changing needs of these newcomers. Sending the money to the city in the form of block grants would allow more effective expenditure and would improve both the physical and procedural infrastructure and allow newcomers to settle better.

Such a list can go on and on. There is a huge number of issues where the city is the key point of service delivery, where it has greater knowledge and experience, or where it can exercise the flexibility and responsiveness that leads to better delivery of goods and services. But the city cannot structure its own solutions, because these solutions must pass the test of acceptability by a level of government with less specific knowledge, experience, or motivation.

Politics

The political barriers to cities having more control of their own destinies are manifold. The two principal ones are Quebec and Quebec. The sovereignty aspirations of some Quebecers have created constitutional gridlock in Canada for decades. Nothing will change the way we govern ourselves unless Quebec perceives some benefit in it for itself. And any change that appears to benefit Quebec will be met with much resistance by the other provinces.

The federal government dance with Quebec has created a dynamic of all the provinces grasping for money and powers from the central government. This has become the dominant, and deafening, discussion of government in Canada. Any attempt to raise the issue of self-determination for cities, even of greater autonomy, barely stands a chance of being heard above the din of "fed-prov" relations. Former Ontario premier Bob Rae, a veteran of constitutional talks, was asked at a Canadian Urban Institute talk about the prospect of a constitutional role for cities. After a brief pause, he said, "Don't hold your breath." He went on to say that there was so much tension and pressure around federal-provincial issues that any attempt to alter or add to the discussion would cause all to be lost, at least in the opinion of the people at the constitutional table.

Another contributing issue is the rural bias of electoral distribution. As Canada has become more urbanized over the course of this century, voting power has not followed people to cities as quickly. Thus, urban ridings tend to have many more voters than rural ones. That makes the vote of an urban dweller count for less than that of a rural dweller. This gives rural voters a disproportionate sway with governors and predisposes governments to focus more on issues which meet the needs of rural communities. One need only look at the issues in provincial elections and notice the absence of urban issues like air quality and transit. And it is often the case that city dwellers elect candidates from different parties than the rest of the province: a Liberal and NDP Toronto in Conservative Ontario; a Liberal Montreal in Parti Quebecois Quebec. One observer of cities has suggested a charter challenge on electoral distribution by city dwellers who find themselves underweighted at the polls.

It is a rare politician willing to cede power and the threat to the power base of provincial premiers is a crucial barrier. If the main cities in each province enjoyed more autonomy, significant political power would accrue to their leaders. Already the mayor of the amalgamated city of Toronto can boast having received more votes than any political leader in Canada's history. Even the person who ran second in that election got more votes than anyone in history except for the newly elected mayor. (In parliamentary democracies, of course, party leaders are elected in their own ridings, not by the country at large. The new city of Toronto encompasses many such ridings, so all the votes added together far outstrip even the biggest riding in the country.)

If the mayor of Toronto had real power, like the power to raise revenues and make expenditures without fear of senior government override or offset, he could harness the economic and social power of the city in a display of political might which could outmatch the best the province could muster. Which premier would welcome that? Which premier would want to be the one who made the mayor of Toronto more powerful, practically, than the premier?

Today, most Canadian cities have a "weak mayor" system. That is, the mayor formally has little more power than a councillor. But the mayor does chair council and has more to work with in terms of the prestige of office as well as more staff, visibility, and resources. There are two important attributes a mayor should have: a vision of the city; and an ability to work with people. Some mayors have one of the two attributes and can get by on that basis. Great mayors have both and combine them to build coalitions to move toward their vision of the city. But the weak mayor system limits a mayor's ability to move as quickly and decisively as may be, from time to time, desirable. The absence of party systems in municipal politics, as is generally the case in Canadian cities, also tends to make the mayors less powerful than in situations where party discipline can be exercised.

Finance

At a Canadian Urban Institute debate some years ago, where the topic was "Should Toronto Secede?," planner and writer Joe Berridge, speaking in the affirmative, made the following offer: give us our freedom and we will continue to export the same amount of capital, indexed to inflation, to the rest of the country. The country, he argued, will be as rich as ever and Toronto will be much, much richer because it will be able to control its destiny and meet its needs.

Economist Enid Slack would concur. Her work has revealed a number of relevant facts: that the city creates more wealth than the non-urban regions and hence is a net exporter of capital; that development costs increase as you move from the centre outwards; that the needs of the city are not met through a process of higher government collection of revenue and the subsequent transfer of wealth back to the city by a trickle down through the provinces.

Some would go so far as to suggest that Toronto's ability to generate wealth is actually constrained by its lack of political autonomy. They would argue that the city would prosper if it was released from the constraints its current subservient status imposes – a gain which could, in turn, be shared by the rest of the country.

It's not that Toronto doesn't want to do its fair share for the rest of Canada. The issue is – how do we create a balance in terms of our resources and responsibilities in a way that doesn't just look good on the trade charts for the city region, but has some impact on how money is distributed among people within Toronto in a way that's consistent with our vision of equity for the country and for the city?

Anne Golden

The dilemma facing Toronto is how to realize those conditions that would allow it to meet its own social and economic needs more directly and more effectively. In aid of this, we convened a gathering of community leaders and posed three questions: Do the conditions exist for Toronto to take greater control of its destiny? What are the models of governance we might consider? And finally, what would be the political paths to gaining greater autonomy?

That gathering, in taking stock of Toronto, noted the great achievements of the past in city building as well as the present opportunities before the urban region. But it also noted today's risks and challenges: deteriorating and inadequate infrastructure; the growing gap between rich and poor, the visible symptoms being hungry children and homeless people; uncertain politicians; and shifting jurisdictions.

There are many of us in this region committed equally to economic prosperity and social justice. We know we can build a society embracing both – not sacrificing one for the other. Senior governments appear to have abandoned the pursuit of peace, order, and good government for the Toronto region. It is time to undertake the struggle on our own behalf.

Alan Broadbent is a philanthropist and businessman,
Chairman and CEO of Avana Capital Corporation,
Chair of The Caledon Institute of Social Policy,
and Chair of the Canadian Institute of International Affairs.

The Evolution of Toronto

David Crombie

I'm now sixty-three years of age, and I have been going to meetings where the evolution of Toronto was talked about for a very, very long time. Sometimes I went by myself, sometimes I accompanied my parents. I was thinking that fifty years ago this month, in 1949, we had just come through a very tough campaign where we saved West Toronto from going wet. All the Tories and all the socialists from Swansea got together to defeat the Grits who wanted to make it wet. It was also in 1949 they first started to dig for the new subway.

It was a time when there was concern that the outer suburbs needed water and we needed proper transportation in and out of the city possibly in the form of expressways. The questions were asked: What do we do with all these large and small municipalities? How do we bring them all together in some governance? These questions began to began to be addressed in the next couple of years.

A decade later, in 1959, I was also going to meetings, because at that time I was a student, earning my living washing cars and chauffeuring for City Hall at the old River Street garage. I didn't chauffeur very often because I didn't chauffeur very well. But I was a hell of a washer – that is where I spent most of my time and on late nights, when the chauffeurs wanted time off, I used to drive the Board of

Controllers and the mayor and the chairman of Metro. They were very proud in 1959 because they were doing two things for sure. One, the Gardiner Expressway. That was a high moment of progress. And of course, Nathan Phillips was winning his battle to build the new City Hall. A project which, in my own judgement, turned the minds and hearts of Torontonians to a different perspective of who they were. Then in 1969, I met Jane Jacobs and watched as she helped to stop an expressway.

There is a point to this rambling introduction. We have been going through changes for a very long time and we will continue to do so. I thought that what I would do is put these changes in some kind of order. Most of them are known to all of you. Singularly, you accept them, understand them, and deal with them. But when you bring them all together, they are really quite remarkable.

One of the most interesting jobs I've had in my life was when I was the Minister of Indian and Northern Affairs in Canada – a job for which I was eminently unsuited. As you know, when they fill the Cabinet in Canada, the Prime Minister of the day looks over the crop of people who were elected and, by dint of their education, their experience in life, and their inclinations, assigns the jobs that best suit those talents. I was born and raised in downtown Toronto and was therefore deemed perfect for Indian and Northern Affairs. I knew so little about the job that I felt I needed to go and talk to people. I spent the next two-and-a-half years doing just that – they were the happiest two-and-a-half years of my life because I learned so much about the country and about people.

I also read a great deal at that time. One of the people I read was Hugh Brody – he's an Englishman who normally writes about the Arctic. But he wrote a wonderful book called *Maps and Dreams* which is about the Beaver people in the interior of British Columbia. The book is interesting because he examines the habits of the Beaver people in one chapter and then moves into a theory about those habits in the next chapter. The whole book is organized in this fashion. About every sixteen pages, there is a series of squiggly lines that look like spaghetti. These are the biographic maps of the Beaver people – the biographic and community maps. For centuries, these maps were constantly changing as they performed the function of telling the Beaver people where the game is, where the fishing is good, where the enemy might be, where (depending on the change of seasons) they can find safety, etc. They are the survival maps, always changing, for the Beaver people.

I think we are like the Beaver people. As we go through various changes, we should ask ourselves "what does this change mean to our own biographic and community maps?"

First, consider the economic map of Toronto. In my lifetime and certainly before that, the economic map of Toronto has been changed absolutely and fundamentally in terms of its wealth creation. In fifty years, it has transformed itself. And it's not just a theory – go around the city and you will see those changes. Stand in front of the Prince's Gates and, as you're looking west, turn north, look to the right, and there you'll find mostly vacant land. Thirty years ago, that was the home of companies like Massey-Ferguson (producer of farm machinery for the world), Inglis, and Pattersons – companies employing tens of thousands of workers for generations. Go to the south end of Etobicoke; twenty-five years ago Goodyear was still there, Guinness was still there – today, they're all gone. The south end of Scarborough – Johns Manville and others.

And as you go around the city, you will see how fast and how fundamental the economic change has been. I was thinking about the waterfront the other day and I remembered the industries that were situated there. Tip Top is still there (although it is destined to relocate) as well as the sugar company, but that's about it. These changes are not the sorts of things you should write off and not think about. There has been an extraordinary change in the economic basis of this city and it affects individual people. When you change the economy you change work. And work shapes the city. It shapes the people in it. It changes our expectations and our understanding of what we need to do to get ahead and get along.

I was riding the subway not too long ago when a fellow came over to me who obviously knows one of my kids. "Mr. Crombie, how are you?" he asked. He was all dressed up in his three piece suit with his little bag going downtown. I asked, "What are you doing now that you're out of school?" He said, "Well, I'm just going downtown." I asked, "What did you take at school after you left Lawrence Park?" He said, "I took engineering at University of Toronto and I just finished my MBA." Then I asked, "Where are you going now?" and he replied, "I'm looking for work." In my generation, if you had shown up in the marketplace with either an engineering degree or an MBA, you'd have no problem. What it does to people's understanding of what their life is going to be about and what their expectations are, are direct results of that economic change.

The second change which has occurred everywhere is a demographic change. This city has taken in seventy thousand new people from all around the world every year for over fifty years. This has absolutely transformed the basic commodity of the city forever and has also reinforced our old immigration patterns. It started in the nineteenth century. A book called *Gathering Place: Peoples and Neighbourhoods of Toronto 1834 - 1945* is worth looking at because it demonstrates that the immigration pattern for Toronto was established long before 1945; that the whole idea of cohabitation in the sense of not requiring either assimilation or segregation was entirely a pattern developed in the nineteenth century, and the big immigration after the Second World War reinforced all of that. The multicultural element was deep in the history of nineteenth century Toronto.

In addition to the immigration and movement of people around the world to Toronto, there has also been a gender revolution. This dramatic change has taken place since the sixties. In a short space of time, we changed the conditions of who showed up to the workplace, who stayed at home, and therefore the conditions of what life was about and how it worked.

Further, in terms of the demography of the place, we have been experiencing the "boomers." As John Kettle pointed out in his book *The Big Generation*, for fifty-odd years they've marched through, reorganizing all the urban furniture to suit their needs. So there's been a demographic revolution along with an economic revolution.

Finally, I think it is worth mentioning that we've absolutely changed our minds in terms of the importance of the environment of the city. There's been a revolution in environmental thinking and action begun by the thinkers. In 1961, as some of you will remember, Rachel Carson's book *Silent Spring*, kicked it off. Ian McHarg wrote a wonderful book called *Design With Nature*. Jane Jacobs linked ecology to the city. William Hollingsworth Whyte wrote a terrific book called *The Last Landscape* and, a little later on, in 1984, came Ann Spirn's book, *The Granite Garden, Urban Nature and Human Design.* And I would add Michael Hough, who's done a great deal in terms of writing about city forms and natural process. The thinkers, then, laid out a framework of new understanding. But there were also "actors" at work in the city such as Pollution Probe in 1970, Greenpeace, the campaigns to save the Don River and the Rouge River, and so on.

The thinkers, the doers, the activists all had a message: they wanted to remind us of the connectedness of things in the building of the city. We could no longer simply treat economic, environmental and community issues separately. We had to deal with them together. I can remember when we first brought out a map of Toronto at the Waterfront Regeneration Trust that I'm connected with. Our environmental map of Toronto, of course, started at the top at the Oak Ridges Moraine, went over to the Niagara Escarpment, and came down to the lake. That whole area is really the environmental map of Toronto. The environmental revolution of our time has already changed corporate understanding of the city in terms of their strategies and marketing. It has also affected individual behaviour as well as government policies and programs. Along with the change in economy and the demography of Toronto, and the change in understanding the relationship of the city to the environment, we've had a change in our political map – we have changed our understanding of what the role of government is. This debate will go on because the recent change in what that role is repeats a discussion which took place a hundred years ago: What is the role of government and how should it change to suit a new century?

We've also had changes in our understanding of jurisdiction and accountability. We have been, in this city, metropolitanising since 1953. By this, I mean we've tried to find ways in which we could deal with both regional and local issues and concerns at the same time. It wasn't a single event; it began in 1953 with the creation of the Municipality of Metropolitan Toronto to deal with primarily transportation, sewage, and water issues. In 1957, I think it was the police. In 1962, the social services. We have metropolitanised for the past thirty-five years and will continue to do so through the Greater Toronto Services Board and the new city of Toronto.

In a fairly short period of time, these four revolutions – economic, demographic, environmental, and governmental – have raised the question: How have we responded? We've responded in two ways. First of all, many people concerned about whatever event was bothering them simply went out to try and fix things. Two different projects I've worked on in the past seven or eight years have demonstrated this to me. The first is the Waterfront Trail which runs four hundred kilometres around Lake Ontario. It has about twenty-five municipalities, seven conservation authorities, endless numbers of businesses and organizations that've been involved in one way or another with eighty projects which have resulted in the development of the trail. The purpose of all those projects is to bring the issues of ecology, economy, and community together. It's been an enormous undertaking by people undirected by a single government. Who owns the Waterfront Trail? It's owned by the whole of the network, not one single government or one entity.

The second project is the Olympic bid. For the last two-and-a-half years, the committee preparing the Olympic bid has brought together the issues we thought were important in order to explain to the public why Toronto should place a bid to host the Olympics. What was really interesting to me was that people got involved with it, and still do. In fact, we did a poll about a year-and-a-half ago which indicated that 80 percent of the people in Toronto supported the bid. Last winter, after six months of incredible stories in the media about scandals in the Olympics, we went back to Toronto and held the poll again. The numbers hadn't budged one bit. It was quite amazing.

When we first went out to talk about the Olympics, we asked people why they thought there should be an Olympic bid and why they would be a part of it. Their responses, indicating five criteria that should be met in a Toronto Olympic bid, are constructive to me because they're part of the core of the civic culture of Toronto. First of all, the proposal should be inclusive, it should be a wide enough ring for everybody – anybody who wants to participate should be able to – and all of the diversity of Toronto should participate in it. Second, it should be socially responsible. Third, the proposal should be environmentally progressive. Fourth, it should be financially sound. And finally, it should leave a legacy.

Whether it's the Waterfront Trail or the Olympics, or some other project, there are tens of thousands of people who are unconcerned about the nature of relationships among governments, but who care deeply about the issues that are before them. The Oak Ridges Moraine still needs to be saved. The Gardiner/Lakeshore corridor issue needs to be addressed. There is the question of the homeless. We have real, substantive issues that concern people. And these people are participating and responding to the changes in their lives in a way that even outmatches the things I can remember in the previous three decades.

I think it might be helpful for me to finish off with my own understanding of the basic organizing ideas that animate people today in dealing with the economic, environmental, demographic and governmental changes. They're not so different from the organizing ideas of the city of Toronto throughout most of its history.

First of all, this city understands the importance of pursuing economic development. Now that may sound obvious, but very often we forget the need for this, especially in good times. If people are comfortable, they tend to think that economic development is not really important. It is a powerful human instinct for people to adapt to their needs. It's why people came to Toronto. It's why they will continue to come. It's why they will stay – if we do what's required for economic development. To maintain the strength of our local economy in the face of global competition is absolutely fundamental to us and people understand that. They are looking for us to do those things that are required to accomplish this. People want us to tackle questions like: How do we organize government? What used to be government? Should there still be government? How do we create a fund or infrastructure? How do we get a self-start? People expect that we're going to do what's required to strengthen the local economy.

You can't get autonomy or make a credible claim for autonomy unless you have some kind of visibility. The most striking thing about Toronto is that it has almost nil political visibility. In my long years in Ottawa, I doubt that the word "Toronto" ever appeared in the index in Hansard.

Richard Gwyn

Secondly, even though people find that having the

opportunity to look after the needs of themselves and their families is paramount, they also feel that the livability of the city and specifically, their community, is important. They understand that communities and neighbourhoods are not simply physical places, they are psychic spaces where human personalities are developed and where basic human questions are raised and answered: Who am I? Where do I belong? What do I believe? These are questions that are answered in small places and spaces.

And thirdly, people will increasingly tell you about the importance of personal security and public order in this city. It's always been a part of Toronto's civic culture and Torontonians still understand that it's not simply social peace we require, not simply the absence of conflict. We want an increasing presence of equity and justice for our people.

I think it is key for us to remember the importance of cities. It was Jane Jacobs, thirty years ago or better, who said, remember that human beings are the only city-building creatures in the world and that the wealth and benefits of society come from the wealth and benefit of cities. I've tried to explain as best I could what I think animates this city, has animated it, and why I think these are still the organizing ideas of this city. If you get frustrated over the next few years trying to change the city and it doesn't change quite as fast as you want it to, I leave you with a thought from Allan Lamport who said, "Always remember that Toronto is a city for the future, and always will be."

David Crombie is a former mayor of Toronto and member of the House of Commons. He is currently the Chair of the Waterfront Regeneration Trust.

There's No Need to Sit and Wait for a Handout

Joe Berridge

Nearly every Monday morning, someone from our company has to wait in an enormous lineup at Pearson International Airport to go through U.S. immigration. They are not alone. The Greater Toronto Airport Authority reports that, since the North American Free Trade Agreement was signed, air travel across the border has increased at almost double the rate of traffic within Canada. It's a visible symptom of the fact that Toronto's economy is becoming North Americanized.

Business in the Golden Horseshoe not only accounts for half of the province's economy – and almost one-third of the nation's – it is very heavily based on exports. Half of the United States' consumer market and more than half of its manufacturing firms are within one day's trucking distance, so it comes as little surprise that more than 90 percent of the exports go south.

Canada, meanwhile, offers Toronto little room for growth. The city is already home to more than half of the country's corporate head offices, all five major banks and the Toronto Stock Exchange, which processes 89 percent of the nation's stock transactions.

So here's the paradox: Toronto can help to keep Canada economically dynamic only through greater integration with the U.S. economy.

To do so, however, it must go head to head with some very substantial cities south of the border that are in the midst of a renaissance spurred by massive reinvestment.

At the moment, Toronto is the continent's third or fourth most important financial centre, its second biggest live-theatre location, and its second or third largest film production centre. Its universities, particularly the associated medical research institutions, compete continually for staff and research funds with the best in North America. The automotive sector remains a major pillar of the regional economy, directly responsible for one in every six jobs in the greater Toronto area. Maintaining our ranking in any of these areas – in the face of well-capitalized U.S. urban competition – will require both a strategy and a scale of public and private financial investment not now evident.

All the work that the economists have done has indicated that the Canadian economy is not terribly important to Toronto any longer. It's the North American economy that's important.

Colin Vaughan

The recent debate over bank mergers captured the need for a new concept of Toronto's future. If the goal is to ensure continuing bank competition within Canada, mergers are a bad thing. However, if the goal is to have the city play a role in global financial affairs, they're probably essential.

A similar future confronts the TSE. Rationalizing the responsibilities of Canadian stock exchanges is a sensible thing to do, but for Toronto to have a stock market of any significance outside the country will require a much more ambitious strategy, possibly including mergers with foreign exchanges to create something that can counter the power of New York.

Similar strategic choices, between a strictly Canadian interest and those of a global city-region, face Toronto with respect to airlines and telecommunications.

Considering that it has invested so little in itself for a decade, Toronto has done remarkably well. We have been lucky – a relatively young postwar city in infrastructure terms still well served by a legacy of good public investment in the 1960s and 1970s. We have been the peaceable kingdom. Without underplaying the historical social tensions in U.S. cities, part of the reason for their precipitous decline in the 1970s and 1980s is that they were just a generation older than we were.

The city of Toronto's ability to meet its operating obligations, let alone new capital initiatives, is extremely limited. The consequences of this financial straitjacket are increasingly evident:

• The Toronto Transit Commission operates on a budget that keeps it at the edge of consumer tolerance. Measures to increase transit use can't be contemplated.

• The condition of roads and bridges steadily deteriorates. In 1997, the city's works department estimated $40 million in essential rehabilitation had been deferred.

• The budget seems to have no room for water quality or environmental improvement.

If the greater Toronto area is slipping behind in maintaining basic services, it can hardly match its competitors' investments in infrastructure and urban regeneration.

In a recent report, the Board of Trade provided a useful list of transportation initiatives it recommends for the city-region's economic health. The list included the development of better links to the airports, the use of Union Station as an integrated transit terminal, and the radical upgrading of the intraregional transit system.

Such initiatives are very much the kind of projects financed by senior governments in the United States and Britain. Whether these are the right proposals (they certainly are a good start) is less important than acknowledging that at present we have no way to undertake any of them.

With respect to urban regeneration, there is little room to intervene in areas trapped in redundancy or decay by regulatory, jurisdictional, and ownership tangles, or to assist areas that have become traps for the disadvantaged.

A cold-eyed look at our urban region reveals a large and increasing number of such districts. The port, the older industrial sections of Scarborough and Etobicoke, the arterial corridors of the inner suburbs, parts of the east downtown, the cores of older urban centres now incorporated in the city region, the concentrations of public housing, the decaying stock of 1960s apartment buildings – all of these border on the spiral of decline once so visible in U.S. cities.

Sadly, we have few if any infrastructure projects that speak to the city-region's future (other than the vital plans for the airport) that can get under way this decade. At best, all of our future infrastructure hopes seem tied to a bid for the Olympic Games. We are in the odd situation in which our urban competition has become interventionist, while we remain locked in a neoconservative mindset, suspicious of any public expenditure.

We could, of course, decide not to compete, keep cutting capital budgets and trimming services, and make no big or bold moves, as we have been doing now for more than a decade. Many once-great cities have declined to purely regional stature: Liverpool, Bordeaux, Detroit, St. Louis, Philadelphia, and Montreal. The social and cultural cost to Toronto would be enormous. Our children will choose not to live here.

> *I boil a little bit when I hear the notion that the U.S. has so much to teach us. I don't believe it. Those grants from the U.S. federal government have done a great deal of harm to cities. Some cities have practically beggared themselves.*
>
> *Jane Jacobs*

The second option is to wait for the great bailout, for major urban funding from the federal and provincial governments. In both Britain and the United States, the national governments have taken the lead in urban regeneration. The rationale behind that commitment is as true for Canada's big cities, but the hard facts on the ground are that we are very unlikely to get an equivalent response.

In any event, we cannot afford to wait. If there is anything to learn from the U.S. and British experiences, it is that the collective costs of deferred maintenance of the urban economy can be irreversible.

We must seize the initiative ourselves. After all, Statistics Canada reports that in many respects Torontonians are better off than residents of "non-urban" Canada (the rest of the country minus Vancouver and Montreal). We make more money (an average annual household income of $60,110 versus $46,405) and are more likely to be university educated (18.8 percent of us have degrees versus 14.5 percent elsewhere).

If we're so smart and so rich, why is our city so broke?

The fundamental strategic goal for the Toronto area must be to become financially self-sufficient, not only from an operating perspective, but also generating a significant proportion of the capital requirements for new investment.

We need a strategic vision that defines Toronto's needs as a North American and global city in the same way that our competitors have been doing so effectively. Three questions should be asked about any new capital project for it to become a priority:

- Will it increase the city or region's productivity and competitiveness?
- Will it improve citizens' long-term quality of life?
- Can it be financed largely on a user-pay basis?

Productive investment has to be distinguished from mere municipal consumption. Indeed, rather than more roads and sewers and recreation centres, Toronto's most important new infrastructure priorities could be a new freeway to the U.S. border for trucks only, a new department of bioengineering at the University of Toronto, and a replacement for embattled Livent Inc.'s theatrical presence here.

We also have to decide what activities the city-region should not finance off the tax base, scrutinizing all the operating municipal service businesses – electricity, water and waste water, garbage, transit – and creating new organizations largely able to meet their own needs.

Toronto is one of the few world cities that still operates these services as main-line businesses. The ability to use the very substantial asset values and cash flows of these municipal businesses is perhaps the only financial option to provide the city-region with what is unlikely to be obtainable from other sources: its own pool of reinvestment capital.

Such an urban infrastructure fund would have remarkable leverage potential, both from public-sector pension funds and from other private-sector institutions.

The federal and provincial governments could greatly assist the effectiveness of such a fund by granting it the tax exemptions, depreciation, and tradable tax credits characteristic of U.S. cities. Asking for this "soft" tax money might be a lot more palatable than requesting grants, especially in a post-deficit public-accounting world. Such techniques have been thoroughly tested by other cities and, while largely foreign to the Canadian and Ontarian fiscal traditions, are commonplace in our real urban economic environment.

Toronto also desperately needs the management capacity for urban regeneration that is characteristic of every other world city. We have no development corporations for public/private projects comparable to the agencies typically responsible for transforming waterfront and industrial lands in U.S. and British cities. That Toronto may have had some less-than-perfect experience with such agencies in the past is no reason to avoid the challenge now.

Finally, Toronto cannot remain a competitive global city without the active involvement of the business, financial, and voluntary sectors.

All successful cities have broadened the constituency committed to productive management of their urban future beyond the narrow framework of homeowner-based local politics. Without such business intelligence and community resources, no effective reinvestment plan can be realized. How we achieve this may be Toronto's biggest challenge.

Joe Berridge is a planning consultant and partner in Urban Strategies Inc. This paper is adapted from his company's recent report, "Reinvesting in Toronto: What the Competition is Doing," *published by the Canadian Urban Institute.*

Environmental and Resource Aspects of Self-sufficiency for the Toronto Region

Richard Gilbert

This paper responds to the organizers' observation that "it is the time for some big thinking about our collective future." Specifically, it responds to the organizers' question "do the conditions exist for the Toronto region to take greater control over its own destiny?" The paper does this through the prisms of environmental constraints and resource availability.

This is not what the organizers initially asked me to do (although they have subsequently agreed to what I have proposed). They asked me to provide a paper that would complement Michael Mendelson's piece on the politics of moving to where we might want to go. I have a long-time interest in this matter. I co-led with Jean Pelletier (now the Prime Minister's chief of staff) the early 1980s' quest of the Federation of Canadian Municipalities to secure standing in the Constitution Act. I am presently working with

> *Ultimately, what I'm interested in is finding a way that Toronto can have more control over its own destiny and can take into its own hands the levers it needs to achieve what it can achieve.*
>
> *Alan Broadbent*

Don Stevenson on a book chapter that touches on that unsuccessful mission. I attached more importance to constitutional matters in the early 1980s than I do today.

Now, my position is similar to Michael Mendelson's in that I believe the focus should be on political action within the region rather than on achieving constitutional change. As well, it should be on securing new powers from provincial governments and on making full use of existing powers. For reasons that will become clear, I would propose that environmental and related matters, rather than "priorities from an urban perspective" be the focus of political action.

I would add the further point that municipalities themselves may have been to a considerable degree responsible for their own impotence. They have come to chant the mantra that more government is bad government, overlooking the relative lack of application of this rule at the local level. They have resisted disentanglement and advocated more provincial and even federal subsidies, ignoring the evidence that shared funding arrangements are sure routes to loss of authority. They have bad-mouthed their main source of income (property taxes) when there is good reason to believe that such taxes are no less inequitable or economically counterproductive than other taxes. Indeed, with more emphasis on taxing land than on the use of land, property taxes could be a useful antidote to sprawl, a point I shall touch on later.

I had the luxury of being a late addition to the program and of thus being able to read the highly commendable papers prepared by Meric Gertler, Joe Berridge, and Enid Slack, as well as that of Michael Mendelson, before I began to prepare my own paper. There is little in their papers with which I disagree.

After reading through the other papers, I concluded that my more useful contribution to the Evolution of Toronto forum would be to bring to the proceedings a perspective rooted in appreciation of some environmental issues and resource constraints.

I will argue that the world may be about to change dramatically, and that Toronto's progress as a region will depend on the extent to which it can both insulate itself from the coming changes and secure competitive advantage in relation to them.

Consider two changes in particular: global warming and the beginning of the end of cheap oil.

Global warming is happening. Events during 1998 removed any doubt in this respect. As Chart 1 shows for the northern hemisphere, 1998 was the warmest year during that millennium. It also showed the largest increase in temperature over the previous year.

Chart 1 is a remarkable compilation of data – ice-core data, tree-ring data, and actual temperature measurements – from numerous sources in several countries by researchers at the University of Massachusetts and the University of Arizona, published earlier this year in Geophysical Research Letters. Temperatures fell very slowly during the first nine centuries of the millennium but shot up during the twentieth century, especially during the last fifty years. These recent increases are well beyond anything that could be regarded as "natural" variation.

That human activity is causing the global warming should not yet be asserted with such certainty. The 2,300 scientists of the UN's Intergovernmental Panel on Climate Change have nevertheless concluded there is "a discernible human influence on climate change."

Climate change, especially the kind of rapid climate change we appear to be experiencing, is mostly bad news. Just a few of its effects are:

• more extreme-temperature events, with resulting heat stress and other consequences;

• more extreme-weather events, with resulting damage to people, property, and ecosystems;

• spread of disease-carrying vectors (e.g., mosquitoes carrying cerebral malaria and dengue fever and ticks carrying encephalitis) to new, unprepared areas;

• sea-level rise, from melting of ice fields and expansion of oceans, and consequent inundation of coastal regions; and

• changes in ocean circulation such that, for example, the Gulf Stream no longer bathes northern Europe with warm water and this region's climate becomes similar to those of coastal areas at similar latitudes such as Labrador and Hudson Bay, and a corresponding but less certain effect at Canada's Pacific coast.

The first three of these adverse outcomes, and more, are documented in a recent *British Medical Journal* by a World Health Organization team. The other two are discussed in the climate change literature, including the excellent annual survey produced by

Chart 1. Surface temperature of the Northern Hemisphere from the years 1000 to 2000

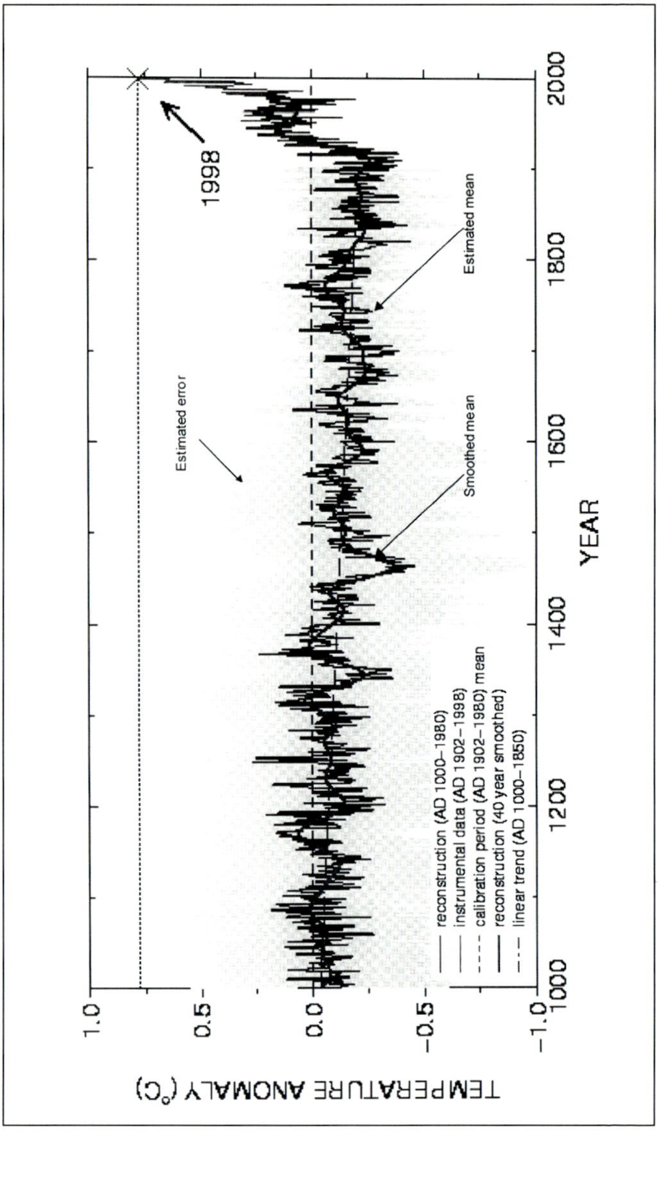

Reprinted from Mann, M.E., R.S. Bradley, M.K. Hughes, Geophysical Research Letters, 26, 759-762, 1999 [copyright American Geophysical Union, 1999]. Reprinted with permission.

Environment Canada. As bad as these outcomes may be, there is worse: the possibility of positive feedback whereby the effects of climate change themselves contribute to further climate change. Here are some possible feedback mechanisms:

• high temperatures disrupt forests to such a degree they store less carbon, thereby raising atmospheric levels of the main greenhouse gas, carbon dioxide;

• high temperatures speed the decay of organic matter in soils, causing higher rates of emission of breakdown products including carbon dioxide;

• high temperatures warm tundra, releasing methane, a potent greenhouse gas.

With positive feedback, climate change could become dramatic to the extent that our planet would not support most present life forms, including humans. The appalling prospect sketched out by William Catton in his book *Overshoot* (University of Illinois Press, 1982) could become a reality.

It is thus becoming apparent that nature must, in the not far distant future, institute bankruptcy proceedings against industrial civilization, and perhaps against the standing crop of human flesh, just as nature had done many times to other detritus-consuming species following their exuberant expansion in response to the savings deposits their ecosystems had accumulated before they got the opportunity to begin the drawdown. Having become a species of superdetritovores, mankind may be destined not merely for succession, but for crash.

You might say, isn't this a bit heavy for a gentle discussion about the future of Toronto? I would respond to the contrary. Many of these happenings are under way or a near-certain part of our future. Global warming is already in progress and we are committed to much more.

It follows there is every reason to reduce fossil fuel use, which is likely the main contributor to climate change; and unless humanity is utterly foolish there will be major attempts to reduce this use. It follows too that regions and businesses that reduce fossil fuel consumption before reductions are imposed will likely gain economic advantage, as will regions and businesses that develop marketable products and skills that help with the necessary reductions, and with adapting to a warmer regime.

Before turning to how economic advantage can be gained let me touch on another prospect of major significance that should guide our strategizing about the evolution of Toronto. It is the prospect of the end of cheap oil, illustrated in Chart 2. Taken from the February 1999 issue of the Centre for Sustainable Transportation's Sustainable Transportation Monitor, Chart 2 shows the following:

• discoveries worldwide of conventional (i.e., cheap) oil peaked in 1962;

• extraction (i.e., world production or supply) of conventional oil is set to peak in about 2003, with an inevitable decline in production thereafter; and

• demand for oil, unless restrained, will continue to grow.

From 2004 onwards, demand for oil will outpace supply. The price will rise, perhaps steeply. Unless demand is restrained, energy costs will rise, perhaps steeply. Oil producing areas will benefit from

Chart 2. The beginning of the end of cheap oil.

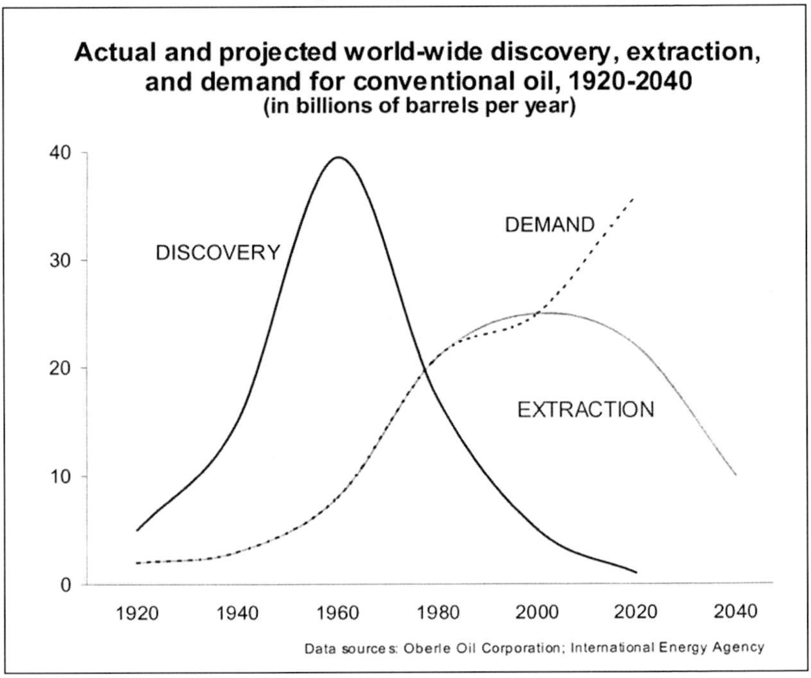

Above chart is taken from Issue No. 2, Sustainable Transportation Monitor produced by the Centre for Sustainable Transportation. Reprinted with permission.

the increased prices. Places such as the Toronto region, which import every drop of fossil fuel, will not. Industries that use large amounts of oil and cannot readily achieve efficiencies, such as aviation and trucking, will fade.

The situation in Canada is unique. Chart 3 shows the following:

- production of conventional oil peaked in 1997; and
- production of other oil, chiefly from oil sands, is now just under a third of all production and according to official projections, is set to comprise more than half of all production in about 2015.

Recent announcements speak to a massive acceleration of production from oil sands that will have most of Canada's oil coming from this source by 2007.

Canada, it should be noted, produces about a third more oil than she consumes. However, about half of our actual consumption is

Chart 3. Production of oil in Canada, in thousands of barrels per day. Actual (1900 - 1995), projected (2000 - 2020), and possible (recent announcements).

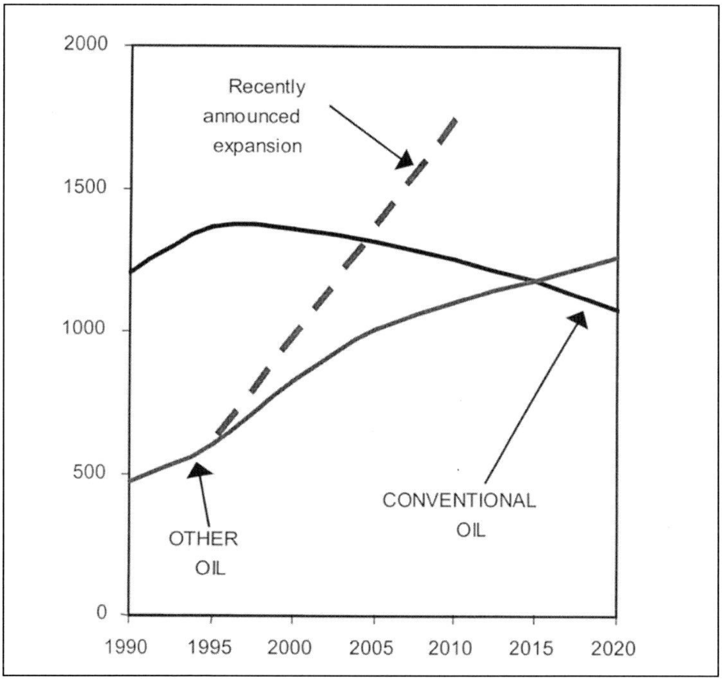

imported from other producers into eastern Canada, which arrangement makes us an integral part of the world oil market.

The oil from oil sands is more problematic even than conventional oil. The massive dislocation of sand and rock produce local devastation. Worse is the energy cost of extraction, which is several times that of conventional oil. As the oil becomes more intractable, the energy required for extraction and processing may even exceed the energy value of the "recovered" oil (much as the synthetic oil produced in Nazi Germany and Apartheid South Africa required much more energy input in the form of coal than was ever produced in the form of oil).

Thus, a car, truck, train or bus that burns gasoline or diesel fuel from oil sands has, in effect, a much higher global warming impact than one burning conventional oil, other things being equal. And we are moving towards much more dependence on oil sands.

There may be a temptation to say that we have a global warming problem mostly produced by oil and the oil is beginning to run out; so what is the problem? The problems, in addition to greater dependence on oil sands, are these:

• much global warming would still occur even if all oil use were to cease tomorrow because of what has already been put into the atmosphere. Moreover, there are many other kinds of fossil fuel (e.g., coal, natural gas) whose use could continue unabated and perhaps increase (The best estimate for natural gas is that its production worldwide will peak in the period 2025-2030.);

• even large increases in world oil prices would have only a small effect on consumption. Price elasticities of oil use are low, especially for the short term. Moreover, retail prices reflect taxes as much as commodity prices;

• high world oil prices will nevertheless drain money from places like Toronto, which produce no oil. Moreover, they will reduce the ability of governments to raise taxes on fuel and thereby generate funds for productive purposes such as investment in benign transport modes and energy efficiency programs.

What is Toronto to do, in the light of the above, to take greater control over its own destiny?

Clearly there must be an overriding preoccupation with reducing dependence on fossil fuel, whether for transport of people and goods, for use in connection with buildings (heating, cooling, lighting) or for industrial processes. This will involve conservation programs, changes in personal and business activity, changes in how land is used, changes in our trading relationships, and development of local energy sources.

Let me touch on what might be the roles of local governments in securing some of these objectives.

Reducing dependence on fossil fuel for transport

No matter what is done elsewhere, Toronto needs to find some way to raise the price of vehicle fuels, both to achieve some reduction in use but also to raise revenue for public transport, bicycle paths, and the like. Raising transport costs can be economically beneficial. For example, as I learned recently in Winnipeg, withdrawal of the Crow's Nest Pass subsidy has led to a surge of food-processing activity in Manitoba. Simply throwing funds at transit could be environmentally unsound. The average bus in the U.S. uses six times as much fuel as the average car, but carries only five times as many people. Other actions must also be taken – conversion of existing road capacity to bus lanes on every route, for example – to ensure shifts from auto to transit use and resulting high transit occupancy levels. Land use changes, described below, will help too.

Reducing dependence on fossil fuels used for buildings

The former city of Toronto initiated a remarkable program known as the Better Buildings Partnership designed to achieve major improvements in energy efficiency. This successful undertaking should be extended throughout the present city and beyond.

Changing business activity

1. As the hydrocarbon century is ending so may be the age of the automobile (and the truck). The Toronto region is among the most dependent places in the world on the automotive sector, and we may have yoked much of our industrial future to a lame duck. During 1999, the chairs of the boards of both Ford (Bill Ford, great-grandson of Henry) and General Motors (John Smith) have predicted the demise of the internal combustion engine as transport's main power source. And yet today it is difficult to see what can replace it, let alone

fuel whatever the replacement might be. The sector is deeply vulnerable. Local government – perhaps the Greater Toronto Services Board – should explore how Toronto's dependence on this sector can be further reduced. At the same time, the GTSB or another body could help us think about how the changing world circumstances could be exploited. Converting the economies of the rich countries of the world into productive, truly sustainable arrangements will involve the greatest investment opportunity in history.

2. One of the more surprising manias of our time is the preoccupation with massive airport expansions in the absence of any evidence that aviation as we know it can continue. There will simply not be the fuel available to support the expanded aviation activity on which the expansions are predicated, and there is nothing on the horizon (except airships) in the way of viable alternatives. Moreover, recent evidence suggests that, compared with automobiles, high-flying aircraft have three times the global warming impact per litre of fuel burned (meaning that an airline passenger's share of emissions during a return trip to Paris is equivalent to more than forty thousand kilometres of automobile use). Few things are more likely to be targeted than air travel when the quest to avert further global warming gets serious. Hitching our wagons to ever-expanding aviation, through investments in airports or the aerospace industry, seems foolish.

Changing how land is used

The Toronto region is shooting itself in the stomach with its wanton gobbling of agricultural land. We become increasingly dependent on imported food just as our supply chains become more vulnerable. Food self-sufficiency for the region and its immediate hinterland may be an unrealistic goal, but for our own security we need to see how far we can go. The Municipal Act may already give municipalities special powers in this regard, a legacy of days when the security of the food supply was taken more seriously. Already the city encourages local production with its Wednesday markets on Nathan Phillips

> *So the question is not whether we are self-sufficient within a Canadian context, but how do we become self-sufficient.*
>
> *Carl Amrhein*

Square. We need to go much farther. Sprawl is costly for us all, as Enid Slack notes in her paper, and it has numerous adverse impacts beyond consumption of agricultural land. Taxation may be a good way to reduce sprawl and to reduce the impacts. Taxing land rather than the uses of land would be a start. Incentives are required too, such as rewarding developers for building near subway stations rather than penalizing them. The Toronto region needs a growth boundary, which would be a visible indication we are taking control of our future. The city of Toronto needs a 20/20 vision for its new Official Plan: a 20 percent increase in its population of people by 2015, to be drawn from growth that would otherwise occur around the city, and a 20 percent reduction in the population of automobiles registered in the city.

Changes in trading relationships

Enhanced communications are making many aspects of globalization inevitable and mostly desirable. Increased dependence on trade may well, however, be something to be resisted in an age when transportation becomes increasingly uncertain. We need shorter supply chains not broader, more vulnerable nets. John Sewell's efforts to facilitate local sourcing were right on the ball. But this kind of work should have the status of a municipal mission rather than rest on the shoulders of one individual. NAFTA is turning out to be an abomination from an environmental perspective. Increases in truck traffic, largely spurred by NAFTA, are now accounting for close to half of Canada's current increases in greenhouse gas emissions, pushing us to be 30 percent or more above 1990 levels in 2010 rather than the 6 percent below these levels required by our Kyoto obligations.

Indigenous energy sources

If we are not to revert to the backbreaking tedium of medieval living, we need energy. The Toronto region has no fossil fuels, but we have lots of sun, a fair amount of wind, quite a bit of garbage that can be turned cleanly into electric power or hot water, somewhat overly discredited nuclear generating facilities (with huge amounts of waste heat that are ripe for exploitation), and, almost uniquely, a deep cold lake that offers numerous possibilities for energy production. The last may be being exploited for cooling – the Deep Lake Water Cooling project of the Toronto District Heating Corporation (TDHC) is presently stalled – but there are many more opportunities. The city of Toronto is moving towards serious management of energy issues through a restructured Toronto Hydro and TDHC, but it has no sense of urgency about the need to secure the region's energy future. And there is almost none of this kind of consideration in the part of the region outside the city, where much more energy is used per capita on account of sparser settlement patterns.

My message is that we are in for convulsive change, particularly with regard to energy use. Taking control of our own destiny means more than ensuring financial self-sufficiency. As a region, we have to be concerned about such matters as energy security and food security. We have to organize our business and other arrangements to reduce our vulnerability to the kinds of change that can reasonably be expected and, where possible, to exploit those changes to our practical and commercial advantage.

Above all, we have to be good global citizens. This means being concerned about the environmental and resource impacts of our actions and strategies, rediscovering our sense of responsibility for future generations, and finding a new moral compass to guide us into the next century – in the words of the Worldwatch Institute, "a compass grounded in the principles of meeting human needs sustainably."

Richard Gilbert is a consultant in urban issues specializing in transportation, waste management, energy systems, and urban governance. He served as a City of Toronto and Metropolitan Toronto councillor for fifteen years and was president of the Federation of Canadian Municipalities in 1986-87. Gilbert headed the Canadian Urban Institute until 1993.

Self-determination for Toronto: What are the Economic Conditions and Do They Exist?

Meric S. Gertler

City-regions have been the crucible of economic development for centuries. Their role has always had many dimensions: they provided a market place for the exchange of agricultural produce; they served as sites for the manufacturing and distribution of goods; they offered a rich variety of services to the consumer and producer alike; they constituted the main repositories for our cultural heritage as well as the principal spaces for the production and dissemination of new cultural products and symbols; they have been centres of learning and innovation; they have acted as sites for financial exchange and control; they have also provided the main platform for social action, the exercise of political power and the conduct of international relations. Cities are uniquely qualified – indeed, defined by their ability – to perform all of these functions, simultaneously.

It is commonplace these days to concede that, because we live in a global economy and an information age, place and geography will soon be irrelevant – that increasingly powerful and pervasive information technologies have become so integrated into our daily lives as producers and consumers that we are now footloose and free to disperse. Moreover, as multinational economic actors and financial markets extend their global reach across national boundaries, so the argument goes, the traditional nation state has become "hollowed out," while localities have been reduced to prostrating themselves to global capital.

It turns out that this commonplace view is inaccurate. A large body of international evidence argues the contrary position: that the importance of city-regions in the global economy has, if anything, increased not diminished. The reasons for this are straightforward. The true hallmark of the current phase of capitalist development is not its global nature (indeed, the case has been made quite convincingly in recent work that the economy was in many important ways more "globalized" one hundred years ago than it is today). Nor is "information economy" the proper rubric. We hear much talk of the "knowledge-based economy" these days and I believe that this concept brings us closer to the mark, for it implies that the foundation of wealth creation lies in our ability to produce new knowledge (invention) and to apply it in commercially viable ways (innovation).

> *Toronto suffers by its status as a subsidiary to the province. This is not simply a Toronto argument, made by Torontonians about Toronto – it has been made equally about Montreal, Vancouver, and other cities in Canada.*
>
> *Alan Broadbent*

However, the concept I like best is the "learning economy," since it conveys not only the central importance of knowledge creation and use, but also captures the essence of what many now argue is the basis of successful innovation and economic dynamism: socially organized learning processes. It also turns out that these social learning dynamics are most prevalent (and effective) when the participants in these learning processes are spatially concentrated. Moreover, virtual interaction (e-mail, voice-mail, etc.) is a complement, not a substitute, for the face-to-face interaction that is necessary to support effective learning between economic actors.

If these arguments are correct, they imply that a city-region such as Toronto might be well positioned to flourish in the era of the learning economy. After all, it appears to have a large, diverse collection of dynamic economic activities. Moreover, its local firms (whether they be manufacturers or service providers) now have easy access to a national and continental market. And as a large and (at least in some parts) relatively dense and well-connected urban region, it offers a rich, fertile substrate on which social learning processes can unfold.

My objective in this brief paper is to outline the conditions for economic self-determination – by which I mean the ability of a region to shape its own economic destiny, to the extent possible within a globalizing economy. Then I wish to consider whether or not such conditions are matched by reality in the case of the Toronto region. A closely related question – and perhaps, ultimately, the more important one – is this: do the present conditions constrain or prevent the economy of the Toronto region from maximizing its full potential? I take it as axiomatic that when we speak of "Toronto" we are talking about an economic entity at least as big as the Greater Toronto Area (GTA), if not bigger. In doing so, I wish to acknowledge the earlier work of others – including, but not limited to, the study conducted a few years ago for the Golden Task Force on the GTA by the Boston Consulting Group (BCG)[1] – which has conclusively shown that city and suburb in the region remain locked in a symbiotic economic embrace. Even though the nature and type of economic relations between them may have changed in recent years, the degree of functional integration remains strong.

In the following discussion, I will focus on four questions. Is the region's economy sufficiently dynamic and productive? What are the foundations for regional economic prosperity in the contemporary economy? Does the region control the levers necessary to implement an effective economic strategy? And finally, are its social and political institutions up to the task?

Economic Dynamism:
What are our "engines" and how well are they working?

It seems to me that the starting point for any discussion about future self-determination of the region must begin by addressing a fundamental question: does the regional economy generate sufficient income to sustain itself, and if so, can it be expected to continue to do so for the foreseeable future?[2] This apparently simple question needs to be broken down into several constituent parts. First, what are the foundations of the regional economy – its "pillars"? Second, do these pillars possess the capacity for innovation and learning that is so crucial to the creation of successful, self-sustaining wealth generation in today's economy?

When considering our economic strengths, it is helpful to have at least a rough-and-ready definition of what constitutes a pillar. My own definition, which takes a sectoral approach, is based on two tests. First, does the activity in question generate products or services which are "traded" – i.e. sold in markets outside the region? Second, do locally-based firms in this sector possess some unique and distinctive capability which is recognized on an international scale? The first test is significant because it tells us whether or not the sector brings income into the region from beyond its boundaries. The second test indicates the presence or absence of successful learning dynamics within the sector locally, giving some vital clues to its resilience and competitiveness – in the dynamic rather than static sense of the term. Using this pair of tests, one avoids having to fall back on tired (and inevitably problematic) dualisms such as "high-tech" vs. "low-tech" or "old" vs. "new" economy.

Toronto's Economic Pillars

In general, the region's economy enjoys a favourable composition of dynamic industries. As the BCG report perceptively noted in 1995, amongst North American city-regions Toronto stood out as having an unusually well-balanced economy. It is strong in both manufacturing and in services (especially higher-order, knowledge-intensive and producer-oriented services). Since 1995, both ends of the economy have continued to grow.

Chief among those strengths are the following:

Automotive

The GTA is home to major assembly plants owned by General Motors, Ford and Daimler-Chrysler. A fourth assembly cluster – Honda's plants in Alliston – lies just north of its official borders, though it is strongly integrated into the region's dense network of suppliers of goods and services. Already strongly integrated on a continental basis before the Canada-U.S. Free Trade Agreement took effect in 1989 (thanks to the 1965 Auto Pact), this sector assembles hundreds of thousands of cars for export to the rest of North America and, to some extent, beyond. Moreover, it appears that the assembly sector has developed a unique capability (supported crucially by the capabilities of the auto parts industry) in the production of minivans – pioneered by Chrysler's Windsor plants, but effectively imitated in Ford's Oakville operations, where the highly successful Windstar was first produced, and in Alliston, where Honda's Odyssey was first assembled.[3] In addition to minivans, the region also produces a number of highly successful passenger sedan models, and its plants score very well on industry-wide quality ratings.

Supporting this superstructure of large assembly operations is a substructure of rapidly growing and increasingly sophisticated producers of automotive parts. At the upper end of a strongly differentiated hierarchy of firms, tier 1 firms such as Magna International supply complete systems for direct assembly into vehicles, coordinating a flotilla of smaller, lower-tier suppliers of subsystems and components. And increasingly, as part of a larger strategy to increase efficiency and reduce unit costs, assemblers have asked their top-tier suppliers to orchestrate more and more of the product innovation process.[4] As a "mature" product (the car) continues to become more and more knowledge-intensive in its composition and production, the region's firms seem well-placed to contribute to its dynamic competitiveness. They have also led the way in introducing new process technologies such as hydroforming, which are likely to become industry standards in the next few years.

Information and Communications Technology

Ottawa-Carleton likes to fashion itself as "Silicon Valley North," while the Kitchener-Waterloo-Cambridge community promotes itself as "Canada's Technology Triangle." Despite these marketing successes – at least as measured in column-inches of favourable reportage – neither of these two hotbeds of development in IT-related industries can match the Toronto region for sheer scale and diversity. Anchored by industry giants such as Nortel Networks (whose world corporate headquarters are in Brampton), IBM Canada, and Celestica, the region's producers of IT equipment run the gamut from manufacturers of a variety of telecommunications systems and computers through to designers and builders of specialty chips (such as ATI), to producers of software for applications in telecom and computing.

The major clusters of activity in this sector are found in relatively suburban settings such as Markham and Mississauga, a geographical distribution which bears some similarity to the phenomenon known as "nerdistans" in technology-intensive regions of innovation and production in the U.S.[5] Despite this industry's apparent preference for locations in the suburban reaches of the GTA, it is crucial to underscore that it maintains strong and vital ties to the central part of the region. According to Markham's director of economic development, who recently discussed his community's strategy for promoting itself as Canada's high-tech capital, "When the economic development office goes courting, it is selling the whole GTA. Toronto's downtown amenities, the universities in the area and the variety of housing are all part of the package."[6]

> *The competition we're facing has nothing to do with U of T or Ryerson. It has to do with the capacity of this region to organize itself to retain and recruit a labour force and all the people that support that labour force in a fundamentally different environment.*
>
> *Carl Amrhein*

Advanced Engineering and Aerospace

Attracting less attention than the automotive and IT industries, but still highly significant, is a group of precision-engineering manufacturers in sectors where quality and performance standards are extremely high. Bombardier's large plant in Downsview is heavily involved in the company's Dash 8 and Regional Jet programs, making a major contribution to the firm's impressive growth during the 1990s. It is also closely linked to literally thousands of suppliers of precision parts and systems, spread both throughout the region and across the continent.

This group also includes a key set of firms producing advanced machinery and production systems for use in the manufacture of a wide variety of other products. The best known of these, Husky Injection Moulding Systems in Bolton, has built a large international network of plants and customers in the highly competitive market for machinery to produce plastic products. It is joined by smaller firms – known as automation houses or systems integrators – which design, build and install specialized manufacturing systems for manufacturers in industries as diverse as automotive, aerospace, electronics/telecom equipment, plastics, fabricated metal products, food and beverage, and others. By offering a local supply of sophisticated capital goods tailored to the needs of the user, the firms in this sector constitute an absolutely essential component of local and regional production networks, making a major contribution to the quality and timeliness of delivery of their customers' final products. Moreover, by combining two technological paradigms – the mechanical and the electronic – this sector produces important innovations in robotics and related automation technologies.

Financial Services

Toronto is well known as Canada's banking capital, with each of the big five banks headquartered here. It is also the dominant centre for investment banking activity and home to the country's largest (and the continent's third largest) stock exchange. While this latter group of activities is certainly not big enough to place Toronto in the top tier of world financial centres, it is firmly ensconced in the second tier along with cities such as Chicago, Boston, and San Francisco. It is highly unlikely that it will ever challenge the New Yorks, Londons, and Tokyos for financial primacy and it would be foolhardy to try. Nevertheless, its future depends on its success as a niche and regional player (where, in this case, "regional"

Look at a city like Boston which has developed a niche in investment and mutual funds as well as insurance. Chicago has a niche in commodities, futures and derivatives markets. Does Toronto have a specialization?

Joe Berridge

may refer to an entire country).

The TSE and the local investment banking industry, for example, have already carved out a relatively successful niche in resource (especially mining) stocks and Canadian-dollar products, and these strengths are likely to be further enhanced with the proposed reorganization of trading responsibilities between the TSE and its sister exchanges in Montreal, Vancouver, and Calgary. Toronto's participation in retail banking has also fared successfully in North America on the basis of two distinctive capabilities – its expertise in developing and managing extensive national branch banking networks, and its pioneering development of on-line systems for banking and discount stock transactions.

Cultural Industries

This diverse group of interrelated activities has rapidly become one of the most vibrant economic clusters within the Toronto region. Like financial services, it is strongly focussed on the central part of the region, where it has blossomed in sectors that include TV, film, video and animation production, music performance and recording, book and magazine publishing, new media and multimedia, live theatre, museums, and the arts. Indeed, the boundary around this eclectic grouping is difficult to draw definitively. One could plausibly include further activities such as specialty foods production, fashion, and the specialty furniture industry. Linkages to hospitality/tourism are also strong. Equally important, particularly for sectors such as new media and animation, are local linkages to specialized software production and, somewhat surprisingly, to sectors such as advertising, banking, telecommunications, and corporate headquarter functions, all of which constitute crucial markets for Toronto's multimedia firms.

What links all of these activities together is a common dependence on the production of images, symbols, and other creative, design-intensive products. In many cases, the source of distinctive capability in these sectors lies in the "cultural capital" that flows from the city's astounding degree of ethnic and linguistic diversity. The corporate heroes include the likes of Nelvana, Digital Renaissance, Alias Research, Livent (in better times), the Royal Ontario Museum, Nienkämper, Alliance Atlantis, and Sullivan Entertainment. But these firms are also supported by a local galaxy of specialized suppliers and subcontractors that include hundreds of small new media production companies and the many anonymous businesses that develop and supply specialty food products for the likes of Loblaws' President's Choice.

Health and Education

Toronto is home to the country's premier complex for medical education and research. Many of its hospitals conduct world-class research in affiliation with the University of Toronto. With the exception of Sunnybrook, these too are concentrated in the downtown core of the region. They are joined by manufacturers of pharmaceuticals (such as Apotex and Novopharm) as well as emerging industries in biotechnology and medical instruments.

These activities should really be understood as part of a larger higher-education complex in the region, which is anchored by three major universities (the aforementioned University of Toronto, York University and Ryerson Polytechnic University) and our equally vital community colleges (some of which, such as Oakville's Sheridan College, have developed internationally renowned educational programs in subjects such as animation). As will be emphasized below, the elements of this sector are crucially important not only for producing the skilled labour needed by other knowledge-intensive sectors in the region, but also for spinning off firms, patents, technological assistance, and other forms of intellectual capital so crucial to ensuring success in a learning economy.

Business and Professional Services

While it is commonplace to regard this class of activities as locally oriented and derivative of the wealth generated by the region's other pillars, this image has to be challenged on at least two grounds. First, this sector provides a range of sophisticated services – from engineering to computer system services, from advertising and legal expertise to management consulting, from scientific testing to specialized logistics, distribution, and telecom services, from accounting to architects and industrial design – which are essential in enabling other local firms to produce and continually update high-quality, design-intensive products. Second, many of these firms have extended their market reach well beyond the Toronto region and southern Ontario – i.e. they too have become "traded" sectors.

Here, Toronto is richly endowed with a deep and diverse pool of local service providers. And the importance of such activities will only grow as two already well-established trends continue to strengthen: first, the preference for manufacturers, governments, and other service providers to outsource more and more of their specialty service needs; and second, the dynamic growth of e-commerce, which has fuelled demand for call centres and electronic forms, and further stoked an already hot market for computer systems design and support services.[7]

Foundations of Success
Local Assets, Global Links and the Mobilization of Capability

It should be clear from the preceding discussion that Toronto's economy exhibits many healthy characteristics. It is still uncommonly well balanced between manufacturing and services production. Knowledge-intensive activities form a strong nucleus – whether in mature or emerging sectors of the regional economy. Moreover, there is compelling evidence that these are highly innovative industries whose products have met the test of continental and, in many cases, global competition.

These pillars also exemplify a key aspect of successful economic regions around the world through the dual nature of the foundations upon which they rest. The means for achieving the successes described above include both local assets and global linkages. The local sources of competitive advantage in a learning economy are now fairly well understood. Foremost in importance is the local capacity to produce well-educated and highly skilled human capital through an education system that is strong at all levels. However, it is equally important to be able to retain this human capital – let's call it by its more familiar name: talent – once it is formed (and to attract it from elsewhere). After all, the higher the level of education and skill attained, the greater the level of actual and potential mobility of the worker. And increasingly, the geography of investment in knowledge-intensive sectors is being driven by the pursuit of capability and talent.

We also know that the key to attracting and retaining talented labour is quality of life, broadly defined to include: the physical attractiveness of a city region's built form; its environmental quality; the richness and depth of other amenities such as its cultural life, restaurants, and the "buzz" of its arts and club scene; the quality of its public school system; and the diversity and depth of employment opportunities for couples in which both partners are seeking work. What is equally clear is that positive feedback processes can kick in to drive the further expansion of such places. Especially for younger workers in knowledge-intensive sectors, what matters most may be the opportunity to "be in a place where there are lots of other people like me." It is probably for this reason more than any other that so many graduates of the University of Waterloo's vaunted programs in computer science and engineering end up not in Waterloo, but in Seattle, San Francisco, and yes, even Toronto.

If capability is the key quality that city-regions aspire to generate and accumulate, then infrastructure should be understood as those local facilities and institutions that mobilize the capabilities of a region's inhabitants and firms. Educational systems can be understood as a key part of local infrastructure. So can providers of specialized training programs and technology transfer centres. Ditto for innovation supporting organizations (university research labs, public and private research institutes, and a well-functioning venture capital market). Of course, we should also add the more physically obvious forms of infrastructure to this list: the high-bandwidth telecommunications networks; the still vitally important transportation networks and facilities for surface and air travel (arterials, highways and bridges, airports); a high-quality public transportation system is also an integral element, since it not only helps reduce surface congestion, but also provides an important travel mode for the journey to work for students and members of the community without access to other means of transportation.

The final local asset on which successful regions consistently rest is the existence of conditions that foster and support social (inter-firm) learning. This form of learning appears to be an increasingly important ingredient in firms' continuous struggle to compete through innovativeness and quality. It provides the opportunity for iterative, interactive forms of innovation as an alternative or supplement to more traditional, linear, private forms of innovation (such as the monolithic, suburban campus-style corporate research and development lab so closely associated with "big science"). In this more decentralized and continuous form of innovation, interaction between technology users and technology producers is key. While much explicit, codified knowledge is exchanged between the interacting parties, really interesting things only happen when more tacit forms of knowledge are transmitted. This process has come to be identified as "learning through interacting."[8]

This implies that there are two attributes required to support rich, dense networks of socially organized innovation processes. The first is a highly articulated social division of labour – in short, a concentration of large numbers of discrete but interacting economic units which, taken together, comprise a larger production and innovation system.[9] As my thumbnail sketches of Toronto's economic pillars made clear, these attributes are abundant throughout the region. The second is the local presence of a set of institutions which support learning through interacting. These could include anything from local chapters of industry associations to specialized technology centres designed to encourage shared learning; from supplier clubs set up by major assemblers to chambers of commerce which provide a forum for regular cross-industry interaction. They also include the rich foliage of opportunities for social interaction found in the bars and supper clubs of Silicon Valley, as well as its local labour market institutions which facilitate the circulation and sharing of knowledge by encouraging relatively rapid turnover and interfirm mobility of employees. I shall return to the theme of social institutions on a somewhat wider scale in a subsequent section of this paper. However, suffice it to say that, on this dimension, I harbour some doubts as far as Toronto is concerned.

While all of these local assets are key sources of competitive strength, they become especially effective when global linkages are also strong. In other words, regions are far more likely to develop innovative capabilities when they remain open to flows of ideas, people (embodied skills, experience, and ideas), investment, and goods and services. Here, Toronto scores very highly. As a major destination for international immigration, it is the beneficiary of net inflows of talent (and distinctive cultural capital) from around the world. In the post-NAFTA era, it is also fully open to flows of investment, goods, and services. For the most part, this is a good thing, although the region did pay an extremely high price from 1989 through to about 1996, as a painful process of adjustment driven by trade and investment liberalization wreaked havoc on many sectors of the local economy.

The essential point here is that we are living in a fool's paradise if we believe that the silver bullet for local economic success is openness alone. If we aspire (as I believe we do) to compete in world markets on the basis of our smarts, our quality, our innovativeness, and our ability to develop new goods and services on a timely basis so that we stake ourselves firmly to a high-income trajectory of economic development, then the nurturing of our local assets is absolutely central to our mission. If we understand local economic development to be a process of mobilizing the capabilities of individuals and firms, and if one of the most important functions of communities is to generate, retain, and attract talent, then this is critical.

Do We Control The Right Levers?

Does the region have access to the powers needed to implement an effective economic strategy?

Having enumerated the elements of a successful regional economic strategy (and suggested that the region's economy is big enough, resilient enough, and sufficiently diverse to generate wealth on the scale needed to bankroll its needs), the natural follow-up question is: do we control the policy levers required to help the region's economy maximize its full future potential and to stay on the high-wage, learning-intensive path to prosperity? The short answer is "no."

A comprehensive analysis of this issue is well beyond the scope of this brief paper. Furthermore, Enid Slack has been asked to address issues of fiscal responsibility and public finance in her paper. However, a number of important points must be made. First and foremost, it is well known that Toronto and the other GTA municipalities – like all other municipal governments in Canada – are the constitutional "creatures" of their provincial master. This legacy of paternalism is one of the oldest and most enduring features of urban life in this country. While the framework for this legacy comes from the British North America Act of 1867, provincial control over municipal affairs – especially finances and planning – has been strengthened by legislative initiative at Queen's Park at key moments in the province's history, beginning with the Depression when many municipalities became fiscally insolvent. It has also been strengthened by the expansion of the province's fiscal capacity primarily through the provincial income tax.

What does this mean for the management of Toronto's economic prosperity? For starters, it means that the responsibility for managing the quality of life in the region is split between local (including regional) and provincial governments. Cities fashion their own official plans (subject to provincial approval), but must work within a framework of basic infrastructure decisions on sewer and water systems, highways, and public transportation networks for which the province controls the purse-strings or sets policy. While cities may wish to free up vacant brownfield industrial sites for new development, their desire to kick-start the regeneration process is constrained by provincial environmental legislation which sets standards for soil toxicity and liability. As my colleague Joe Berridge will no doubt point out, the scale of investment needs for the refurbishment, renewal, and expansion of basic infrastructure is considerable. Finding the ways to finance this investment (and to make sure that investment decisions have due regard for quality of life in the region) are major challenges for local government in the GTA.

In the crucially important field of education, the city's dilemma is especially poignant. On the one hand, as I have already pointed out, from a strategic point of view there is absolutely no doubt as to the crucial importance of investing in human capital formation at all levels of the education system. And yet, with the province's recent reorganization of expenditure and revenue-raising responsibilities for K-12 education, local municipalities within the GTA have effectively lost control of the single most important policy lever for economic development. Even if their citizens wish to impose higher taxes on themselves in order to dedicate more resources to their local educational system, they are now prohibited from doing so. Instead, they are faced with a "one size fits all" approach which is set and imposed by the province, regardless of local variations in preference or need.

Similarly, responsibility for the financing and development of the region's innovation-supporting organizations (including colleges, universities, hospitals, and public research institutes) is shared between the provincial and federal governments. While the province provides the lion's share of funds for capital and operating costs and determines policies and priorities for post-secondary educational programs, the federal government plays a key role through its control of our national research councils (Social Service Health and Research Council, National Science and Engineering Research Council, and the Medical Research Council) which disburse funds to bankroll research in universities, hospitals, and research centres. Once again, the outcomes for Toronto have been mixed. While the region benefitted tremendously from the provincially driven expansion of the university and college system during the 1960s, it also suffered from the same governments' failure to support this system adequately through the 1990s. By all objective indicators, Ontario's universities have been significantly underfunded in comparison to those in the rest of Canada and to those publicly funded institutions of comparable stature in the United States. While recent moves to shore up provincial funding – at least in fields deemed as high priorities by the province – and the recovery from early-1990s' cuts to the federal research councils' budgets are positive developments for the Toronto region, these actions also vividly underscore our continuing dependence on senior levels of government for the financing and control of key public components of the region's innovation infrastructure.

More generally, while the province is the most obvious senior actor in this discussion, it should be said that the Feds assert their influence on the innovative capability and dynamism of the GTA in less obtrusive – but no less important – ways. Although not framed as "urban" policies, these federal initiatives have each in their own way exerted a major influence over development in the region. I have already alluded to the crucial significance of the 1965 Canada-U.S. Auto Pact, whose production-sharing provisions created the framework and impetus for a wholesale rationalization and expansion of the assembly and parts-producing sectors in the GTA and across southern Ontario. The Free Trade Agreement has also had a profound influence on the competitive environment for the region's economy, even if the jury may still be out on the question of the net bottom line for job creation and wealth generation in the GTA.

Banking policy – set largely by the Feds, although with a significant provincial role in the regulation of securities trading – continues to shape the size and nature of financial services activity in Toronto. While some lament the recent federal decision to prohibit domestic bank mergers, believing this to have negative long-run consequences for the city's banking sector, this too must be acknowledged as a highly contentious and complex area for debate.

Finally, we must recognize the tremendous significance of federal (and, to some extent, provincial) cultural policy (and, of course, federal immigration policy) on the development and growth of Toronto's cultural economy. Policies designed to bolster the production and dissemination of Canadian cultural products (by setting CanCon requirements for radio and television programming, or by providing direct financial support and investment incentives for film and TV production, book and magazine publishing, and other means of support for the arts) have, along the way, spurred the development of major media and arts industries in Toronto. They have also created the foundations to support the now rapidly growing multimedia sector in the region.[10]

In sum, it is clear that most of the key policy levers for shaping the economic trajectory of the region are not directly controlled by local (or, where they exist, regional) governments in the GTA. In some cases, such as in education, this is the source of real and probably justifiable frustration at the local level. In other cases, it is reasonable to ask whether or not it makes sense for local governments to control the levers in question, such as those which shape the innovation-supporting infrastructure of the region. I shall leave these kinds of questions to my learned colleague Enid Slack. However, I wish to emphasize one key point here: namely, that it is foolish or misguided to presume that, just because city-regions have become the key locus for innovation and learning, they must now be expected to provide the full wherewithal to support these activities themselves. If one looks at many of the world's great clusters of economic activity, the influence of senior (especially federal) governments is almost universally very strong. While this is most obvious in great capital cities like London and Paris, it is equally true of places like Silicon Valley, which has risen, fallen, and risen again at least in part on the basis of national defence policy and military procurement in the U.S., and whose high-tech firms show more than passing interest in federal anti-trust and competition policy.

The State of our Social and Civic Institutions:
Is Toronto a Learning Region?

When one surveys the experiences of the world's most successful economic regions (whether they be true city-states such as Singapore and pre-1997 Hong Kong, or less autonomous forms such as Silicon Valley, southern California, Germany's Baden-Württemberg, Italy's Emilia-Romagna, and others), one is struck not only by their sheer innovative dynamism and wealth-generating potential, but also by another characteristic: the quality and focus of their social and civic institutions. While it is notoriously difficult to prove a conclusive link between economic development and the quality of institutions, a large and rapidly growing international body of work in economics, political science, geography, planning, sociology, and other social sciences is converging on the central idea that institutions matter a great deal.

This literature suggests that several attributes of local institutions are key. The first is what might be called "reflexivity," by which I mean the process of engaging in critical self-reflection in order to foster the continuous improvement of the regional economy and its quality of life. To be most effective, this process must be conducted in an open, transparent, democratic, and participatory way. Continuous improvement of this sort may arise through two different aspects of reflexivity: the ability to diagnose a region's own weaknesses and strengths accurately; and the ability to identify successful practices in other regions and transpose them back to the home region – i.e. to learn from elsewhere.

Flowing directly from this analysis, the concept of the learning region has emerged to describe those places that provide the right institutional environment to encourage both private and social learning at four different scales, three of which I have already discussed: the individual worker, the individual firm, and groups of related firms. The fourth scale of learning, then, is found within the governance mechanisms themselves.[11] Hence, the role of the region-state (including both public and private sector institutions) is to animate the formation of interactive relationships between individual firms, and between firms and the kinds of regional institutions described earlier. However, such regional agencies and institutions should also be thought of as learning organizations themselves, in that they lead and facilitate the collective process of critical self-assessment, and they actively seek to emulate and learn from the successful experiences of counterpart organizations and strategies in other regions and nations.

Moreover, these regional institutions play a key role "in sickness and in health" – that is, not just in helping the success stories become and remain so, but also in helping regions recover from adversity and setbacks. Hence, one finds examples of such institutional animateurs playing key roles in Silicon Valley in order to deal with some of the less desirable side-effects of success (e.g. traffic congestion, labour shortages, housing affordability) and to ensure that the region's firms continue to meet emerging competitive challenges. One also finds these organizations spearheading the drive to restore a declining regional competitive edge in places like Baden-Württemberg, whose machine-tool and automotive industries encountered serious difficulties in the early to mid-1990s, for the first time since the end of the Second World War. Similarly, in chronically lagging regions such as Wales, local organizations of this sort have enjoyed significant success in helping to convert a classic branch-plant economy into something resembling a learning region, in which large, foreign-owned manufacturers have been encouraged to grow deeper roots into the Welsh economy through closer, more collaborative relationships with local suppliers and colleges.

On this dimension, I fear that Toronto does not at present fare terribly well. The formation of effective, reflexive civic institutions of the sort described above implies a further characteristic that has not been made explicit thus far, but which is notoriously elusive in the GTA: a strong unity of purpose through the recognition of, and focus on, common goals for economic and social development. It also implies the existence of governance mechanisms whose spatial scale corresponds to the boundaries of the full regional economy. Here too we fall well short of the mark.

On the positive side, we have enjoyed a strong history of institutional innovation – most importantly through the establishment and evolution of Metropolitan Toronto – which has likely made an important contribution to the region's economic prosperity by providing a rational scale for planning and decisions pertaining to infrastructure investments, by pooling and spreading the benefits of growth region-wide, and by creating a single, integrated tax jurisdiction. We have also produced effective private sector governance organizations such as the Toronto Area Industrial Board which made significant contributions to this process by promoting a GTA-wide vision for economic development.[12]

On the negative side, the region has seen the emergence and entrenchment of deep internal political divisions which sap its energy and prevent it from achieving the kind of unity of purpose I have just described. The origins of this problem may well lie with the political fragmentation of the region through the province of Ontario's creation of the regional municipalities surrounding Metro Toronto in the 1970s. This has had at least two unfortunate consequences. First, it accentuated political and social differences by creating parallel (and rival) power structures without the benefit of an overarching governance structure to promote region-wide decision making and consciousness raising. Second, discrepancies in provincial funding formulas for education and infrastructure, along with local variation in assessment practices, differentiated between Metro and its surrounding neighbours, creating substantial differentials in tax rates for industrial and commercial property. This not only produced a much stronger centrifugal influence on employers (particularly manufacturers) within the region, but also fuelled a process of intra-regional competition for employment and investment which most analysts agree is unproductive, wasteful of scarce resources, and has probably served to reduce the region's overall appeal to potential incoming investors.

This has already proved a tough legacy to overcome. As these local political divisions become further entrenched, they amplify the continuing economic, social, and cultural divergence between the area codes of 416 and 905. And this divergence feeds back to accentuate still further the political differences, as the stark divisions within the region's political geography demonstrate in the recently concluded provincial election. Despite the creation of a Greater Toronto Marketing Alliance with a mandate to present a unified face to the rest of the world (and especially to potential investors and employers), and the birth of the Greater Toronto Services Board to promote region-wide decision making with respect to infrastructure and transportation, we are still some distance away from having a truly integrated structure for the management of economic development in the region. Furthermore, the present politics of division and discord, plus the reluctance of the province to alter the status quo in any fundamental way, do not augur well for the future. Even though we remain one functional – though perhaps increasingly less well functioning – economic region, unity of purpose may be our most scarce commodity.

> *Political autonomy for Toronto? That's impossible. The senior governments will never give it up. No governments will ever give anything up. Except that, of course, the impossible happens all the time in this country.*
>
> *Richard Gwyn*

Meric S. Gertler is the Goldring Professor of Canadian Studies Department of Geography, and Director of the Programme in Planning, at the University of Toronto

Notes

1. Boston Consulting Group (1995) The Fourth Era. Toronto: study prepared for the Task Force on the Greater Toronto Area.

2. Note that I am not asking, at this point, "do we produce enough tax revenue – under local control – to pay for the various public goods required to ensure our continued competitiveness?" While I will address this question, I leave a fuller discussion of the issue to my colleague Enid Slack.

3. Significantly, the Odyssey is now being exported back to Japan, where it is marketed as the Lagreat.

4. This constitutes a decidedly positive development for the Ontario and GTA automotive industry, whose assembly sector has traditionally remained notorious for performing very little research and development in the province.

5. This term, coined by Joel Kotkin in a recent *New York Times* article, refers to suburban enclaves of technology-based firms and their workers' residences, epitomized by places such as Irvine in southern California.

6. Quote attributed to Stephen Chait, in an article by Ijeoma Ross, "High-tech firms log on to Markham," *The Globe and Mail*, Tuesday, June 1, 1999, B12.

7. For recent evidence on the explosive growth of employment in these sectors, see Bruce Little, "New jobs in unheard-of places," *The Globe and Mail*, Monday, May 24, A2.

8. The classic works in this field include E. von Hippel (1988) *The Sources of Innovation*, (New York: Oxford University Press); B.A. Lundvall (1988) "Innovation as an interactive process: from user-producer interaction to the national system of innovation," in Dosi, G. et al. (eds.) *Technical Change and Economic Theory* (London: Pinter Publishers) pp. 349-69; and B.A. Lundvall and B. Johnson (1994) "The learning economy," *Journal of Industry Studies*, 1, 23-42.

9. According to AnnaLee Saxenian, the social organization of economic activity clearly differentiates Silicon Valley from other agglomerations of microelectronics and computer production such as Massachusetts' Route 128. While the former can attribute much of its technological dynamism to its open, dispersed and highly interactive forms of inter-firm organization, the latter suffered stagnation and decline in the 1980s and early 1990s because of its local firms' obsession with secrecy, self-sufficiency, and vertical integration. See her 1994 classic *Regional Advantage: Culture and Competition in Silicon Valley and Route 128*, (Cambridge, MA: Harvard University Press).

10. For a more complete discussion see S. Brail and M.S. Gertler (1999) "The digital regional economy: emergence and evolution of Toronto's multimedia cluster," in H-J Braczyk, G. Fuchs and H-G Wolf (eds.) *Multimedia and Regional Economic Restructuring* (London: Routledge), pp. 97-130.

11. See for example R. Florida (1995) "Towards the learning region," Futures, 27, 527-536; and K. Morgan (1997) "The learning region: institutions, innovation and regional renewal," *Regional Studies*, 31, 491-503, for a broader discussion of the learning region concept.

12. See the recent Ph.D. thesis by Betsy J. Donald (1999) "Economic Change and City Region Governance: The Case of Toronto," Department of Geography, University of Toronto, for a more detailed presentation of these arguments.

The Road to Financial Self-sufficiency for Toronto: What are the Impediments and How Can They be Overcome?

Enid Slack

We learned from Meric Gertler's paper that Toronto's economy exhibits many healthy characteristics but that local governments in the Greater Toronto Area (GTA) do not control the policy levers required to help the region's economy maximize its full future potential. One of the policy levers over which municipalities have limited control is municipal financial tools. Because cities in Canada are creatures of the provinces, provincial governments can create or destroy municipalities, allocate expenditure responsibilities to municipalities, and determine what taxes they can levy. Provincial transfers, which provide financial assistance to municipalities, are often prescriptive in terms of where the money is to be spent and what standards need to be met. Provincial governments set rules for municipal borrowing for capital purposes and require that municipalities do not run a deficit in their operating budget. In short, municipalities have limited flexibility in financial matters.

This paper looks at the Toronto region from a public finance perspective. The first part summarizes expenditure responsibilities and sources of revenue for GTA municipalities as a whole to illustrate that the region is not financially self-sufficient. The second part then identifies five major impediments to self-sufficiency and suggests how these impediments could be overcome. The third part describes the inability of the GTA to operate as a region from a fiscal perspective and the long-term implications for financial sustainability.

Expenditures and Revenues of Municipalities in the GTA

In 1997, the most recent year for which a consistent database is available on revenues and expenditures in Ontario, municipalities in the GTA (regional and local governments combined) spent almost $7.75 billion on operating expenditures and over $1.8 billion on capital expenditures.[1] Table 1 on page 56 provides a breakdown of expenditures by function.[2] On the operating side, the largest expenditures were for general welfare assistance (at 15.7 percent of total expenditures), followed by general government (12.5 percent), transit (11.5 percent), and police protection (10.7 percent). Overall, social and family services, which are mandated and cost-shared with the provincial government, accounted for 22.3 percent of the operating budgets of municipalities. This means that municipalities have limited control over about one-quarter of their operating budget. On the capital side, the major municipal expenditures were for transit (24.5 percent of capital expenditures), roadways (20.9 percent), sanitary sewers (14.4 percent), and parks and recreation (10.6 percent).

Since municipalities are not permitted to incur a deficit in their operating budget, operating revenues are roughly equal to operating expenditures. In 1997, total operating revenues in GTA municipalities were $7.74 billion. Operating revenues come from a number of different sources, as shown in Table 2 on page 57. The main source of revenue to municipalities in the GTA, as elsewhere in Ontario, is the property tax. It accounted for 45.8 percent of operating revenues in 1997. The next largest source of revenue is provincial grants at 21.1 percent, most of which are conditional in that they have to be spent on functions designated by the provincial government. User fees accounted for 16.1 percent of local government revenues in the GTA and other revenues were 9.2 percent. Own-source revenues

Table 1: Distribution of Operating and Capital Expenditures, All GTA Municipalities, 1997

	Operating Expenditures (%)	Capital Expenditures (%)
General government	12.5	5.3
Fire	5.0	1.2
Police	10.7	2.2
Conservation authority	0.2	0.3
Protective inspection and control	1.4	0.1
Subtotal protection to persons and property	17.5	3.9
Roadways	5.9	20.9
Winter control	1.0	0.0
Transit	11.5	24.5
Parking	1.1	0.5
Street lighting	0.4	0.2
Air transportation	0.0	0.0
Other	0.1	0.0
Subtotal transportation services	19.9	46.1
Sanitary sewer system	5.5	14.4
Storm sewer system	0.1	0.6
Waterworks system	5.0	9.7
Garbage collection	1.4	0.2
Garbage disposal	1.6	1.3
Pollution control	0.1	0.0
Other	0.0	0.6
Subtotal environmental services	13.7	26.8
Public health services	1.5	0.6
Public inspections and control	0.2	0.0
Hospitals	0.0	0.2
Ambulance services	0.9	0.1
Cemeteries	0.0	0.0
Subtotal health services	2.6	0.9
General assistance	15.7	0.5
Assistance to aged persons	3.0	1.4
Assistance to children	0.4	0.0
Day nurseries	3.1	0.2
Subtotal social and family services	22.3	2.0
Parks and recreation	6.5	10.6
Libraries	2.5	1.2
Other cultural	0.9	2.4
Subtotal recreation and cultural services	9.9	14.2
Planning and development	1.7	0.6
Total	100.0	100.0

(total revenues less grants from other levels of government) were $6.1 billion.

On the capital side, the main sources of revenue were contributions from reserves and reserve funds (which are comprised of property taxes, development charges, and user fees set aside for capital purposes), provincial and federal grants and loan forgiveness, and municipal borrowing.

Based on this information on revenues and expenditures, it is clear that municipalities in the GTA as a whole are not financially self-sufficient. Local fiscal imbalance occurs when revenues fall short of expenditures. When measured by operating expenditures less own-source operating revenues, local fiscal imbalance shows the ability of GTA municipalities to meet expenditure requirements from their own revenue sources. On the basis of expenditures of $7.75 billion and revenues from own sources of about $6.1 billion, the local fiscal imbalance in the GTA is approximately $1.65 billion or almost $400 per capita. It is anticipated that, with increased responsibilities at the local level combined with the current wave of property tax freezes across the province, this fiscal imbalance could worsen.

Table 2: Sources of Operating Revenues, All GTA Municipalities, 1997

	Revenue (%)
Property taxes	45.8
Water and sewer billings	5.0
Subtotal taxation	50.9
Payments in lieu of property taxes	2.7
Municipal support grant (unconditional)	1.9
Other provincial grants (conditional)	19.2
Total provincial grants	21.1
User fees	16.1
Licenses and permits	1.4
Contributions from reserve funds	2.8
Other revenue	5.0
Subtotal other revenue	9.2
Total revenue	100.0

Impediments to Financial Self-sufficiency

Local fiscal imbalance occurs essentially because there is a mismatch of expenditures and revenues at the local level. This imbalance tends to increase over time because local revenue sources tend to grow more slowly than income, while local expenditures tend to grow more quickly. This imbalance can, in principle, be rectified either by increasing the sources of local revenue or by reducing local expenditure responsibilities.

There are currently five impediments to financial self-sufficiency in the Toronto region: the sharing of social service costs between provincial and municipal governments puts an undue burden on the property tax; provincial restrictions preclude municipalities from sharing provincial income, sales, or fuel tax revenues; under-utilization of user fees at the local level results in inefficient use of services and increased demand for services; a lack of funds for municipalities to invest in capital means that infrastructure needs are not being met, with implications for attracting businesses and revenues in the future; and the mounting costs of sprawl have increased both capital and operating costs at the municipal level. To remove these impediments, some will require a provincial government (or a federal government) response while others will require municipalities in the GTA to make different financial decisions in the future.

Provincial/Municipal Sharing of Social Service Costs

The local services realignment in Ontario in 1998 (more commonly referred to as downloading) resulted in the transfer of responsibility for many "hard" services (such as water, sewers, roads, and transit) plus social housing and increased responsibility for social services to municipal governments.[3] In return, the province took over the funding of elementary and secondary education and cut residential property taxes for education in half.

This realignment contradicts the advice given by every committee, task force, and panel commissioned in this province over the last decade to sort out responsibilities between the provincial government and municipalities.[4] Based on solid public finance principles, these reports all said the same thing: social services should be funded entirely by the province. Indeed, Ontario is now one of only two provinces in Canada that still require municipalities to fund social services – the other province is Manitoba.

Why should social services not be downloaded onto municipalities? First, social service programs, such as welfare assistance, redistribute income to the poor. It is more appropriate for the provincial government to redistribute income using the income tax than it is for municipal governments to fund these services using the property tax. Even those of us who have long extolled the virtues of the property tax do not believe it is appropriate for the property tax to fund social services! In other countries where social services are a municipal responsibility, the main source of revenue is not the property tax.[5] In Stockholm, for example, local governments provide social assistance, education, and health care. The primary source of tax revenue is the income tax which funds almost half of local expenditures. Revenue sharing is used in Frankfurt whereby the city benefits from a share of the income tax.

Second, municipalities do not have the tools to fund welfare because they cannot borrow funds to meet operating deficits. This means they will be under great financial pressure to reduce welfare payments when the need increases. Let us not forget that Toronto's economy is booming right now. A recession would significantly impact the city's ability to provide services. In the current fiscal environment of zero property tax increases, the result is more likely to be reduced social assistance payments and other municipal services than a property tax increase.[6]

Third, social services require uniform standards to be applied across the province. Indeed, the provincial government does set the standards for service provision. The problem is that it does not pay all the costs. Municipalities have to pay part of the costs but have limited flexibility in terms of how the service is provided.

A key factor in moving Toronto along the road to greater financial self-sufficiency is to "upload" social services and social housing to the province. As David Crombie said at the time of the transfer, "it is wrong in principle and devastating in practice" to download social services and social housing to municipalities.

Provincial Restrictions on Other Revenue Sources

The province determines what revenue sources can be tapped by municipalities. In Ontario, municipal income and sales taxes are not permitted at the local level. Although there are problems in levying local income and sales taxes (such as the high costs of administration and the ability of taxpayers to shop in other jurisdictions to avoid sales taxes), municipalities could piggyback onto the provincial income tax as is done in Manitoba. Sharing provincial sales tax revenues has also been recommended by the Pichette Commission in Montreal on the grounds that sales taxes provide a direct link to economic activity.[7] Sales taxes are not currently being shared between provincial and municipal governments anywhere in Canada. If municipalities in Ontario are increasingly responsible for social services, sharing the income tax should be explored.

As part of the local services realignment, the province transferred responsibility for transit to municipalities and increased responsibility for highways. Toronto now pays for transit entirely at the fare box and out of property tax revenues, with no provincial grants. Indeed, this is one service that is financially self-sufficient. It is strapped for funds, however.

The transit system and regional transportation functions in greater Vancouver were transferred from the provincial government to the Greater Vancouver Transportation Authority (now called TransLink) in July 1998 by an act of the B.C. legislature. TransLink receives a share of provincial fuel taxes collected in greater Vancouver. A tax on motor fuels earmarked for transportation construction and improvement makes good economic sense. An earmarked fuel tax of this nature is similar to a user charge that charges road users the costs of providing services. The ability for municipalities to receive a share of the fuel tax (and possibly licence fees and other transportation-related charges) to fund road or transit improvements would increase Toronto's financial self-sufficiency and its ability to pay for transit and transportation needs in the region.

Under-utilization of User Fees at the Local Level

The efficient provision of goods and services requires local governments to charge directly for services wherever possible. In this way, the user of the service knows how much it costs to provide it and can make an efficient and informed choice on how much to consume. User fees allow businesses to know how much they are paying for the services they are receiving from local governments. Based on the services provided and the cost incurred, they can make an efficient decision about where to locate.

User fees are charged in GTA municipalities for transit, water and sewers, recreational activities, and other services. They make up about 16 percent of revenues collected. They could be extended to cover more services, however, such as garbage collection. Furthermore, where user fees are charged, "proper pricing" is not generally applied. A good example is water pricing where water rates are frequently applied at fixed charges independent of the volume of water consumed.[8] The result is over-consumption of water and over-investment in water capacity. When prices are set at less than the marginal cost, large water consumers are favoured such as those with large lawns and swimming pools. The problem is further compounded by sewer surcharges being pro-rated on the water bill.

There is also a critical link between pricing and investment decisions. If prices are set too low, demand will expand to the point where facilities become crowded and there is pressure to expand them. If capital costs are financed out of general revenues, then they appear to be virtually free to consumers. If proper pricing is used, then investment decisions will be based on what people are willing to pay for the service.

If user fees were used more widely and social services were funded by the province, the role of the property tax would be restricted to financing those services of general benefit to people in the community that cannot be priced (such as parks and street lighting). This would remove pressure on the property tax and increase local financial self-sufficiency.

Lack of Funds to Invest in Capital Infrastructure

In his paper, Joe Berridge emphasized the inability of the city of Toronto to invest in new capital initiatives and how this has led to its falling behind its competitors in maintaining basic services. Obviously greater use of user fees, as noted above, would alleviate pressure on the property tax and also reduce the demand for some types of infrastructure. Berridge suggests some interesting roles for the federal and provincial governments in providing tax incentives for infrastructure investment.

There are two ways in which the federal government could assist municipalities in providing the needed capital infrastructure. The first is to establish a partnership along the lines of the Infrastructure Works Program in which the costs of the program were shared equally by the federal, provincial, and municipal governments. Municipalities selected the eligible capital projects subject to provincial approval.

Second, the federal government could provide tax incentives to stimulate investment in local infrastructure funds, along the lines proposed by Joe Berridge. In this way, federal funds could be used to lever funds from the private sector. It is sometimes easier to ask the federal government for tax incentives than for direct spending. The main problem with tax incentives, however, is the leakage to those who set up the funds. A dollar of investment often means only fifty cents actually goes towards infrastructure.

Federal or provincial grants and tax incentives would provide additional funds for municipalities to invest in infrastructure but they will not make them financially self-sufficient. Municipalities are permitted to borrow to meet capital requirements but, interestingly, over the last twenty years the rate of borrowing has declined significantly in Ontario municipalities. Indeed, most municipalities are well below provincial borrowing limits. Since the benefits of capital infrastructure extend into the future, it seems both fair and efficient for future residents to share in the cost of financing these projects.

The Mounting Costs of Sprawl

Urban sprawl significantly increases the cost of services, in particular infrastructure. Findings of the GTA Task Force indicated that, if development patterns in the GTA continue as they have over the past twenty-five years, an additional $55 billion of capital investment will be needed over the next twenty-five years for roads, water, and sewer infrastructure.[9] An additional $14 billion will be needed for operating expenditures. With more compact urban development in the GTA, the task force estimated that over $12 billion in capital costs could be saved over twenty-five years and these savings do not include reducing the costs of pollution, policing, parking, and other costs.

I just keep asking myself, where are the roads and mass transit and the sewage and water lines going to go if we don't plan on a wider basis?
John Crispo

Reduction of urban sprawl can reduce the costs of services and thereby increase the financial self-sufficiency of the Toronto region. Furthermore, the financing tools used to pay for growth have an important influence on how the growth will occur. Studies on development charges (levies charged by municipalities on developers to pay the growth-related capital costs associated with development) show that the design of the charge can influence land use patterns.[10] Charges based on average cost pricing whereby all developments within a particular municipality pay the same charge per lot regardless of location, for example, actually promote sprawl. Since all developments pay the same charge regardless of the costs incurred by each individual development, there is no incentive to locate near existing services. Marginal cost pricing (where charges reflect the cost of each development) are neutral with respect to the location of development.

Inability of the GTA to Operate as a Region from a Financial Perspective

Meric Gertler's paper mentions the lack of unity of purpose in the GTA and how that hampers its ability to function as an economic region. From a municipal finance perspective, self-sufficiency of the region depends on the fiscal strength of each of the municipalities in that region. As Neal Peirce notes in his book, *Citistates*,[11] there are close ties between centre city and suburban economic performance. The financial strength of the region depends on the success of the central city and the suburbs.

The establishment of the Greater Toronto Services Board (GTSB) is a good start. So is the pooling of social assistance, social housing, and transit costs in the GTA. Pooling has been politically contentious, however, and some regions are expressing interest in pulling out of it. But the GTSB should be doing more. It should be setting spending priorities for these services in a way that reflects the needs of the entire region. It is necessary to develop region-wide policies for housing, land use, and transportation, together with a social balance that reverses the trend towards growing urban/suburban polarization. I have to agree with Meric Gertler, however, that the entrenchment of deep internal political divisions makes this unity of purpose difficult to achieve.

Inter-regional competition for businesses is another example of the lack of unity of purpose. Property tax differentials across the region have exacerbated this problem. High business taxes have often been cited as the reason why businesses have left what is now the city of Toronto to go to suburban municipalities in the GTA. This exodus has left what the Board of Trade has termed the "hole in the doughnut" or, as I like to think of it, a "hole in the croissant," given the geography.

Historically, there have been many reasons for the higher taxes on businesses in Toronto. Some have argued that costs are higher in Toronto so tax rates overall are higher. Others have argued that provincial grants for education have left Toronto with no provincial funds for education and thus has resulted in the higher property taxes. A third reason is that the assessment system has discriminated against commercial and industrial properties and in favour of residential properties throughout the province but more so in Toronto than anywhere else. In short, commercial and industrial taxpayers in Toronto have been subsidizing single-family homeowners much more than in other GTA municipalities.

The property tax reform of 1998 has resulted in a uniform province-wide assessment system based on current value (which is just another name for market value). At the same time, however, the provincial government has permitted municipalities to use tax rates to maintain the discrepancies between property classes. Table 3 (below) illustrates the differential treatment of properties by showing municipal transition ratios. These are the ratios of commercial property tax rates (and industrial property tax rates) to the residential tax rate in each of the regions in the GTA. In Durham, for example, the tax rate on commercial property is 1.4214 times the rate on residential property. Even after property tax reform, Toronto's tax rates on commercial and industrial property are significantly higher than in the surrounding regions.

Table 3: Municipal Transition Ratios in GTA Municipalities, 1998

	Commercial	Industrial
Durham	1.4214	2.9817
Halton	1.4565	2.3599
Peel	1.2971	1.5986
Toronto	4.2759	5.9685
York	1.1190	1.3427

The provincial takeover of education funding has been accompanied by a lowering of the provincial rate of tax for education on non-residential properties in Toronto (and other municipalities in Ontario that are above the provincial average) over an eight-year period. This means that taxes on commercial and industrial property in Toronto will slowly come into line with its suburban counterparts. This will take time, however. In the meantime, the tax rates on commercial and industrial properties are higher in Toronto than elsewhere in the region.[12]

Financial sustainability requires that the GTA works together from a municipal finance perspective. This means continuing to share the costs of region-wide services such as social assistance, social housing, and regional transit and perhaps sharing the costs of other region-wide services as well, such as waste management and regional roads. Furthermore, a uniform property tax rate on non-residential property, at least for education, would significantly reduce inter-municipal competition for industry and employment. In short, municipal financial tools need to be used to support the reality that the GTA is one economic unit.

Enid Slack is an economist and is President of Enid Slack Consulting Inc.

Notes

1. It is anticipated that these estimates will be somewhat different for 1998 following the transfer of responsibilities from the province to municipalities. These data are not yet available, however.

2. Tables 1 and 2 were derived from data provided by the Municipal Finance Branch, Ministry of Municipal Affairs and Housing, Ontario.

3. Regional pooling of social service and transit costs in the GTA has spread the impact of these changes throughout the region.

4. See, for example: "Hopcroft Report" (1991); "Fair Tax Commission Report" (1993); the "Report of the Greater Toronto Area (Golden) Task Force" (1996); and the December 23 letter to the Minister of Municipal Affairs and Housing from the Crombie "Who Does What" Panel (1996).

5. See McMillan, M. 1997. "Taxation and Expenditure Patterns in Major City-Regions: An International Perspective and Lessons for Canada." In Hobson, Paul, A.R. and France St-Hilaire. *Urban Governance and Finance: A Question of Who Does What*, p. 42.

6. The swap of services also has implications for the future. The provincial takeover of education funding in a period of an aging population will reduce its expenditure demands. At the same time, the social service demands on municipalities will increase.

7. Task Force on Greater Montreal. 1993. "Montreal: A City-Region."

8. See Bird, Richard, M. and Thomas and Tsiopoulos, 1996. *User Charges for Public Services: Potentials and Problems.* Toronto: International Centre for Tax Studies, Faculty of Management, University of Toronto, p. 25.

9. Greater Toronto. 1996. "Report of the GTA Task Force," p. 111.

10. See, for example, Slack, Enid. 1994. "Development Charges in Canadian Municipalities: An Analysis." Toronto: Intergovernmental Committee on Urban and Regional Research.

11. Peirce, Neal. 1993. *Citistates: How Urban America Can Prosper in a Competitive World.* Washington, D.C.: Seven Locks Press, p. 19.

12. It is interesting to note that in the last five years, the city of Vancouver has made a deliberate effort to shift the property tax burden to the residential class in four of the five years since 1994 (the exception was an election year!). This policy was partly in response to the results of a KPMG study which showed that non-residential property uses less services than residential property: non-residential properties pay 60 percent of the property taxes in Vancouver and consume only 29 percent of the services. See KPMG, "Study of Consumption of Tax-Supported City Services," 1995.

The City Status of Toronto

John Sewell

My discussion of Toronto's city status comprises five parts: How big is Toronto?; Form influences behaviour; City stretch and city government; The evil uncle; and finally, Is there nothing to be done?

How big is Toronto?

If we want improved city status for Toronto, what do we set as our boundaries? How big is the city? The answer to this question will define the meaning of any brave new city status.

The problem is one of political cultures. The culture of the pre-Don Mills city is at considerable odds to the post-1950 suburban city, as can be seen by the results of the June 1999 provincial election. All ridings in the pre-1950 city elected MPPs who are opposed to the Mike Harris government; all in the post-1950 city elected Harris candidates.

Residents in each city define their ideas of citizenship, politics, and culture in fundamentally different ways. One side generally exhibits the following values: desires for social justice and programs which create equality; participatory decision-making; high social interaction; and high values placed on cultural and artistic expression. The other stresses individual autonomy, reduced government, and more limited public involvement.

The urban form in which each culture exists is designed to reflect these values (or maybe it reinforces these values), and the municipal governments which represent these cities have structured their programs accordingly.

> *I live downtown but I don't consider myself to be a downtown person. My concern is much more regional.*
>
> *Jane Jacobs*

If the city which has an enhanced status is big enough to include all four million residents of the Greater Toronto Area (GTA), then the post-1950 culture will dominate the city, in the same way that culture now dominates the province of Ontario. Entrenching that culture seems like a dumb thing to do – it doesn't move anything forward.

Many seem to overlook this limitation of a larger city. The Golden Task Force on the GTA assumed that if a GTA were to be created, it would stop building sprawl in short order because of the significant costs involved. It assumed that since large lots increase the cost of servicing, the municipality would require smaller lots; since transit is more cost-effective than travel by private automobile in cities, the municipality would promote transit; and so forth. But that seems to be a false hope. Suburban politicians embody suburban values, and sprawl is high on their list of good things. They have limited belief in the role of public agencies to achieve much of benefit to individuals and limited commitment to using governments to address social problems such as environmental degradation or inequalities of income. They would let developers build sprawling communities if that is how they thought they would make money.

If the city with the enhanced status has boundaries which extend only to the edges of the pre-1950 city (i.e. the former cities of Toronto, York, and East York) then there is some hope such a city would have strong policies about social justice, urban form, culture and artistic expression, and political participation. It might even have some influence on the cities which surround it. But in the scheme of things, the new city's influences would be small, representing a minority of people in the larger city.

These cultural differences can't be papered over by drawing new boundaries and then granting cities new powers. As has been learned with amalgamation in Toronto, new boundaries result in the pre-1950 city being swamped with post-1950 voices – the worst of all possible worlds.

In short, there are big problems assuming that enhanced city status alone will be a benefit to those who want strong policies to stop sprawl, end environmental degradation, or enhance social justice. If the preponderance of votes on the council come from the post-1950 city, that won't happen. Who wants to live in the province of Toronto if its politics are the same as those of Mike Harris?

Form influences behaviour

Some argue that the merit of a self-governing political unit is that it quickly learns lessons that it didn't have to pay attention to when it shared decision-making with someone else. It will learn that some ways of doing things are more expensive than others, and it won't take the more expensive approach.

If only that were so. The problem is that expense is only one factor in decision-making. Habit, bias, and outlook probably play even larger roles. Form does influence behaviour since it shapes the way one looks at space and relationships. Low density suburban form influences the people in that space to favour approaches which limit the public sector and enhance unfettered individual and corporate decision-making.

Thus the cultural problems confronting a larger self-governing city are ones that cannot be overcome by simple education. Bad form makes for bad learning and bad relationships. Suburban representatives are not about to disown the very form in which they exist.

Residents in the pre-1950 city tend to forget this lesson about form. They assume it is normal to support programs which reduce social inequality, which assume wide participation in policy-making, and which allow for a large public realm – but those are simply values which are inherent to and amplified by a city form which includes significant levels of intensity, an active street life, and casual meetings of friends in public spaces. These social values are generated by the specific way the city is built, they do not seep out of the "well-planned" city if it has low densities and uses that are widely separated from each other.

This also means that trying to arrange a rapprochement between post- and pre-1950 political representatives is very difficult. They don't share a lot in common about what they see as the future of city life. One group wants more roads to thread through the city; the other wants a better transit system.

Can they work together? Of course. But they do not form the perfect couple.

City stretch and city government

There seems to be an assumption that the city as an economic entity must be congruent with the city as a political unit. This is not a good assumption, least of all for the reasons already stated above concerning differing cultures.

As we learned during the fight about amalgamation, there are substantial benefits to an urban area which consists of different political units existing in close proximity to one another, benefits which are denied by amalgamation. Different units will adopt different approaches to problems, some of which will be better than others, and good administrators in one unit can learn from others and steal more successful programs. Staff can transfer from unit to unit, ensuring shared experiences. Each unit can develop and protect its own culture, something that is very important to the pre-1950 city, given the dreadful impacts of the post-1950 city.

> *Our upper tier governments have a very restricted capacity to help us because they are carrying enormous costs of accumulated debt that they didn't have in the fifties when they did what was so effective for the short term - twenty to thirty years. These carrying costs are diverting huge sums of money that might be better spent on other things.*
>
> *Carl Amrhein*

What's needed are some ways of linking the various municipal units together to help with joint decision-making. Before amalgamation, this was done in Toronto by Metro, the regional government, although some will claim that Metro was too heavy-handed and not innovative enough in terms of the issues it controlled, including police and welfare. Those criticisms begin to raise the necessity of having regular debate about how different issues get addressed. (It makes sense for the pre-1950 city, which bears the weight of social service problems, to have a larger role in determining appropriate social programs.) Cost-sharing between municipal units will always be an issue, but need not be wildly divisive.

There's no need to ensure that the whole of the city as an economic unit fits within a single political unit. What is needed is some mechanism for regular discussion and decision making by the political units.

The evil uncle

It's never easy making decisions in a family when there is an evil uncle all ready to disrupt things. Evil uncles can take advantage of what seem like the most rational of arrangements.

That's the situation Toronto finds itself in at the present time. The provincial government seems to want to take actions which disrupt decision making in Toronto. Witness the forced amalgamation, the downloading of social and other costs, the imposition of higher property tax rates in Toronto than in any other municipality in Ontario, the proposed reduction in the size of Toronto's City Council, and other punitive actions. Mike Harris is an evil uncle. Toronto was once wealthy because of its own money unlike the suburbs which have relied on provincial grants to fund their public schools and their transit systems.

Strategies for Toronto to raise enough money to regenerate itself (such as selling off capital assets such as the water, sewage, or electrical systems) sound good, but will in all likelihood be frustrated by the provincial government of Mike Harris. If Toronto has money, count on Harris to seize it, or to require (as he is doing with Ontario Hydro) that it be sold at a discount to the private sector.

In the current environment, if past actions are any indication of what will happen in the future, the evil uncle will frustrate any attempt by the big city to deal creatively with its financial challenges.

Is there nothing to be done?

This is a dark situation for Toronto, the big city, to find itself in. The only way forward is for Toronto to link its demands with those of other municipalities towards which the provincial government does not bear so much hostility. One demand all municipalities can agree on is the demand for more autonomy – all want the ability to make their own decisions, without provincial interference, just as they were able to do until 1995. They also want to be protected from provincial decisions to force its financial responsibilities on them. What they require is a statement – perhaps a law – that the province will respect local autonomy and will not change financial arrangements without substantial notice, without full independent impact studies, without prior discussion, and without full discussion in Queen's Park committees and the legislature.

This is an agenda that all municipalities in Ontario can share, one on which they can make common cause. And without this step being taken, any talk about enhanced powers for Toronto is empty.

John Sewell is a former councillor and mayor of Toronto. For the past fifteen years, he has been a writer, community organizer, and commentator on city issues. He writes a regular Citystate column for eye weekly, *a Toronto newspaper.*

The Emancipation of Cities

Michael Mendelson

Cities are the constitutional orphans of Canada. Canada's Constitution recognizes two orders of government: the federal government and the provinces. Urban areas are entirely the creatures of the provinces. Everything about the city per se is at the behest of the province. Should a province decide that cities will no longer have elected councils, no longer have mayors, or pay a special tax for the pleasures of urban living – so be it. Legally, cities have no independent political life aside from that granted to them by the provinces.

What would it take to change the Constitution to give Toronto recognition commensurate with its actual role in the nation, allowing it some independent status and rights separate from the province? The Canadian Constitution provides for a number of different amending processes, some of which require the unanimous consent of all provinces and the federal government (for changes in the structure of fundamental institutions). However, for changes which affect only a single province, the Constitution can be amended by a simple majority vote in the affected province and the Parliament of Canada. It would appear that a change in the constitutional status of Toronto would fall into the latter category and require only a majority vote at Queen's Park and in Ottawa, unless it also changed the nature of federal institutions.

But the impotence of cities is not only legal and constitutional: it is also political. Urban issues are always secondary in the provincial political arena. If a political party is to win a majority in the legislature, it must win representation from both urban and non-urban areas. A political party paying close attention to urban issues would soon lose its support outside of urban areas. Any party focussed on urban issues would therefore automatically define itself as a non-governing party. Much safer to pretend that the province represents a more or less homogeneous whole and talk about "province wide" issues like jobs, health care, and education. Unfortunately, these pan-provincial policy issues rarely address the priorities of the urban area: transportation, homelessness, air pollution, the vitality of street life, and so on.

This is a case of the chicken and the egg. There can be no constitutional change without a political change to permit urban needs to come to the front of the line in provincial politics, but urban needs will not be a winning political issue as long as the current forms of provincial government persist.

So is it possible for cities – and especially the city of Toronto – to escape the trap of powerlessness and achieve an increased measure of autonomy and capacity to address their own needs?

There are three, not necessarily exclusive, potential routes to achieving greater power for Toronto: the traditional route; the establishment of a new governmental entity; and the establishment of a new political entity. This paper explores these three routes, but it does not pretend that any of these offers the definitive solution, or even that better alternatives might not be available than the three set out here. Indeed, I do not personally endorse all of these alternatives. Rather, this paper is meant only as a preliminary contribution, to stimulate thinking and provide some basis for discussion.

The Traditional Route

All of the critical issues facing Toronto must be dealt with by the geographic area known as Greater Toronto Area. Few, if any, serious issues can be addressed by the city of Toronto on its own. The huge need for inexpensive and high quality public transit along with the coming traffic gridlock cannot be dealt with just by

Toronto City Hall. Finding a way to reduce and properly dispose of garbage must be addressed through a plan for the whole urban area. So far as we know, crime and the need for public order do not stop at the borders of Toronto, nor should policing. Housing needs are better dealt with by all parts of the Greater Toronto Area acting together than each attempting to protect its own turf. The air pollution which threatens to choke Toronto is a GTA-wide problem. And the list goes on and on.

The provincial election campaign has been underway for one week as this paper is being written. One of the remarkable aspects of this campaign is what is not an issue: The government's forced amalgamation of Metro Toronto into one city, and its total failure to respond to the need for a political entity for the whole GTA area – an entity which could actually begin to tackle some of the challenges noted above – does not seem to be anywhere on the political radar. Instead, the only vehicle we have to address the issues that will determine the success of Toronto over the next decades and more is a shadowy body called the Greater Toronto Services Board with no direct elections, no clear mandate, no taxing powers, no democratic accountability, and no independent power. It is purpose-built for impotence.

I'm fearful of the future, not only for the area where I'm living, but for the GTA because I don't see any individuals or any institutions around that are going to coordinate all these different levels of government.
John Crispo

So, in the current configuration of city and province, pressing urban issues must be dealt with either at the city level or at the provincial level. But as I have argued, the city level known as Toronto does not have the power to deal with the issues that cross over the boundaries of the amalgamated city, which are just about all the important issues for the city's future. Since there is no viable body at present at the GTA level, the only alternative then is to go to the provincial level. And here is another dilemma, because provincial level political parties take on these issues only at their peril.

Taking the traditional route means plugging away at the provincial political parties in the hope that one or more of them will get serious about urban issues. To do so in a sustained manner would require a long term committed interest group that can put meaningful pressure on parties around urban issues and, more importantly, make these live issues for the electorate since, in the end, parties respond to votes.

The traditional route has the advantage of being clear and simple and well within existing political culture. It is what is expected. It may succeed some day, but it will always be an uphill battle for the reasons already noted – the existing forms of political representation mean that no provincial party wants to become the spokesperson for urban issues and especially Toronto.

A New Governmental Entity

One core of the problem is the absence of an empowered government at the GTA level, so why not focus on creating one? This would mean advocating with the provincial government and the existing municipal entities in the GTA for a new, democratic and empowered form of governance for the whole GTA. The new governance mechanism would have the mandate and the power to deal with pressing cross-GTA issues. Of course, no government is effective and can exercise real power unless it has access to an independent tax source, so this would have to be addressed as well.

Pursuing this alternative would require first working on a proposal for the new GTA government, probably initially in a series of meetings like this throughout the GTA. The next step would be to develop, at least in outline, some key elements of the new governance structure. The final step would be to organize public support and political pressure for the new structure.

> *To say that there are some overriding laws that show things that we can't do, doesn't mean that we can't do all kinds of things within our constraints.*
>
> *Jane Jacobs*

This alternative has the advantage of being possible to approach incrementally, growing a new governance structure from the current structure. It also may be more acceptable to all the current governments, as it is more familiar and since there is a pretty self-evident and pressing need for some means to come to grips with pan-GTA problems. It has the disadvantage of requiring a thousand and one compromises, and the end result may not at all resemble what is actually needed. In particular, without strong political pressure, it is likely that every existing city would jockey to ensure its interests were protected in the new structure, and it is unlikely that the outlying suburbs would voluntarily permit themselves to become part of a political entity in which they were the minority and which had access to their tax base.

A New Political Entity

This alternative would see a new political party formed – say, the Urban Party – which would concentrate almost exclusively on priorities from an urban perspective. It would never get a majority in the provincial legislature, but it might, under the right circumstances, hold the balance of power in a minority House.

Nothing focuses the attention of existing political parties like the prospect of a potentially successful new competitor arising on the scene. Its advantage is that if the Urban Party did succeed in electing even three or four representatives, it would undoubtedly change the focus of Ontario politics. But there are many disadvantages as well:

- forming a successful political party is very expensive and far from assured of success;
- the chances are that the Urban Party could just siphon votes away from other parties with good urban platforms, ironically resulting in the election of the party with the worst urban platform; and
- to work, the party would have to represent a broad coalition, but could such a coalition actually formulate meaningful policies and hold together in the face of competing loyalties?

Michael Mendelson is Senior Scholar
at the Caledon Institute of Social Policy
and a policy consultant for governments and institutions.
He has held several senior public service positions,
including Deputy Minister of Cabinet Office in Ontario,
and has published many articles on social and fiscal policy.

Towards Home Rule for Urban Policy*

David M. Nowlan

By the 1970s, Canada had discovered itself to be an urban nation, a country no longer defined by fishing ports, farming hamlets, and mining towns. To many observers, this seemed to lead logically to the requirement that we have a national urban policy. Accordingly, governments at all levels began uncertainly casting about in attempts to discover what that policy should be. In a short-lived experiment, a federal Ministry of State for Urban Affairs was established in 1972 to help define Ottawa's role in matters that, constitutionally, were principally the responsibility of the provinces.

This official interest in urban issues was in many ways long overdue, but as the expanding federal and provincial bureaucracies wrestled with their concepts of Canada's urban system, I became concerned that we were losing sight of what was being accomplished, city-by-city, at the local level. New waves of politicians, officials and active citizens in Vancouver, Montreal, Toronto, and elsewhere were redefining what constituted a successful city, but they were constantly hobbled by restrictive provincial legislation and, often, by federal practices. What municipalities needed, especially the larger metropolitan areas, was not a vision imposed upon them by senior governments but greater freedom to formulate their own

* From the *Journal of Canadian Studies*, vol. 13, No. 1 (Spring 1978). This paper was reprinted under the title "Towards Urban Home Rule in Canada," in the international journal *Ekistics*, Vol. 44, No. 262, September 1977.

policies in areas such as land-use planning, taxation, and infrastructure development.

The restrictions that then existed on the ability of local governments to formulate local policy continue to exist, and they continue to frustrate the efforts of local governments. In Toronto, they have led the mayor and others to argue that greater Toronto needs the legislative powers of a province. I believe that the best way to persuade senior governments of this need for greater local autonomy is through a careful articulation of the costs of the current constraints and the benefits that would flow from greater legislative freedom. I have tried to do this in a recent article on local tax policy, which I regard as a companion piece to this 1978 article.*

David M. Nowlan, 1999

The Challenge

With almost indecent passion we have come to embrace over the past decade a new Canadian frontier. Canada has discovered itself to be an urban nation with, as constant repetition reminds us, near-80 percent of our population now living in urban areas. The indulgent exploration of our social past, an ardent political present, and the foundation of our economic future all share common ground among our Cabbagetowns and Gastowns, our Scotia Squares and Commerce Courts. Recent witness to this new urbanism has been borne by a steady outpour – from the provinces and Ottawa – of locally oriented Royal-commission, official-committee and task-force reports.

Final and clinching confirmation that Canada's new horizon is not the unclaimed prairie shale or Arctic tundra but redevelopment at Portage and Main is provided by the shifting emphasis of government spending. In a striking reversal of earlier patterns, goods and services and capital spending by local governments across the land has come to exceed – since the mid-1960s – comparable spending by either the federal or the provincial governments. This local expenditure reached

* "Local Taxation as an Instrument of Policy," in Frances Frisken (ed.), *The Changing Canadian Metropolis: A Public Policy Perspective*, Institute of Governmental Studies, University of California, Berkeley, and Canadian Urban Institute, Toronto, 1994, chap. 25, pp. 799-837. This article is available at http://www.chass.utoronto.ca/~nowlan. Just follow the pointer to recent papers.

$11 billion in 1974, close to $2 billion above the total provincial figure and almost $3 billion above the federal outlay on goods and services and capital items.[1]

With urban matters having so recently come to occupy a central position, we are still uncertainly casting about to define urban problems and to establish appropriate urban policies. Amidst this state of confusion the financial imbalance of municipalities threatens to dominate all other considerations, undoubtedly because it is the easiest problem to display and understand.

Between 1950 and 1974, the proportion of local revenue covered by local sources of finance – mainly the property tax – fell from 80 to 53 percent. In absolute terms, the gap between spending and revenue has grown by more than twenty-fold, from one-quarter of a billion dollars to its present $6.2 billion. Most of this increasing shortfall has been covered by transfers from provincial governments and, to a much lesser extent, from the federal government, but the final, net deficit of municipalities in Canada is now about $1 billion a year, an amount that must be met by borrowing in the bond market. Urged on by outside events in recent memory, like New York City's near-bankruptcy, it is thus tempting to look upon urban problems in Canada primarily as crises of finance.

However, the simplicity of this diagnosis is deceptive. To begin with, the element of crisis that bespeaks financial mismanagement is absent in part because of the strict and conservative control that municipalities are legally required to exercise over their budgets. In fact, using accounting concepts much closer to methods in the private sector than to those of other levels of government, local corporations must cover with current revenue all current expenditures. In this sense, no deficit financing is allowed, and what we observe to be a net fiscal imbalance requiring municipal-bond financing is in fact borrowing undertaken to expenditure on capital items only. The terms of this borrowing are subject to firm legislative control, frequently with different amortization periods specified for capital items having different assumed rates of physical depreciation. In place of crisis, there exists a more subtle set of individual issues, some of which may have financial symptoms while not themselves being financial problems.

Compared to the situation ten or fifteen years ago, local governments now rely heavily on financial transfers from senior governments. Barely more than half their current revenue comes from local sources, while close to 90 percent of the remaining share is transferred by other governments in the form of conditional or specific purpose grants.[2] This naturally raises questions about the process of decision-making for urban areas and begins to direct our attention to some unresolved constitutional problems. Increasingly the right to make municipal decisions is available to the highest government bidder, with the result that political responsibility for local matters is drifting rapidly upward. Since this is happening in the absence of any explicit policy and in the face of frequent protestations favouring local autonomy, it must be a matter of special concern.

The absence in Canada of an explicit urban policy was identified by N.H. Lithwick in his 1970 report to the Minister Responsible for Housing as the major urban problem. To fill this policy vacuum, Professor Lithwick proposed a pyramidal, hierarchical approach to policy formation informed by systems-oriented research efforts. He argued that "the possibility of drafting effective urban policies is everywhere prevented by the absence of global development plans." Urban policy demanded, therefore, "a shift in the locus of initiative, imposing on public authorities an obligation to orient, rationalize and plan not only the physical and economic but also the textual character of urban life. The basic approach calls for the development of comprehensive provincial plans that are informed by and compatible with national strategies of social, economic and physical development." He concluded that "if the activities of public authorities are to be directed toward the goal of maximum social and economic opportunity in the urban centres of Canada, they must be conducted in accordance with a comprehensive strategy designed to achieve consistency and common purpose" (Lithwick, 1970, pp. 170 ff.).

This was a tall order, and it came at a time when, from within the larger cities themselves, citizens were beginning to struggle more forcefully at the local level with the very difficult and confusing issues that would shape their cities and their lives. A call for global development plans and national strategies was hard to relate to the local, existential realm of transportation problems, questions of land densities and urban size, and to matters of health and welfare. With the effort it took to understand and resolve some of these problems on the ground, how were we to believe that higher flying national strategies were either possible or desirable?

Such a querulous attitude might conceivably be cut short by the recollection that we are now, according to the figures, an urban nation, with 17 million Canadians living in urban areas. However, these people live in widely diverse physical surroundings. The basic definition of an urban area for census purposes is any municipality with a population of 1,000 or over, but actually less than one third of our population live in urbanized areas of 500,000 and over, and only a little more than one half live in one or other of our twenty-three census metropolitan areas, a number of which have populations barely in excess of 100,000 (Statistics Canada, 1972).

Heavy concentrations of people with relatively low proportions of owner-occupied dwellings are singular features of our larger cities only. It is only in Montreal and Toronto that the inner cities in the urban agglomeration have population densities of almost 20,000 people per square mile. In Winnipeg and Vancouver, the comparable densities are somewhat under 10,000; in Ottawa, 7,000; and so it goes down to the point where inner-city densities, even in some of our metropolitan areas, are less than 1,000 persons per square mile (Statistics Canada, 1973). High densities, high rates of tenancy and large populations oriented towards one central business district define a set of urban, social, and physical characteristics that are not nation-wide although they do apply to a large number of people. It seems, on balance, wise to guard against the presumption that nationally or even provincially promulgated goals filtered down through a hierarchical planning system will ultimately affect our large cities in ways that are either desired or sought after by the citizens of those cities.

These thoughts point towards the creation of more autonomous and better structured local government units, especially in big cities, as a desirable first step in the development of a new urban policy. Why is this so resisted? The answer lies partly, of course, in the unwillingness of senior levels of government to transfer power outside their own jurisdictions. Municipalities, no matter how large or politically sophisticated, operate entirely under the legislative paternity of the provincial governments. They have no constitutional status and very inadequate political mandates to bring to tri-level consultations, where they can hope for little more than some spectator benefit from the federal-provincial sparring matches.

But even more important than this political intransigency is a determined intellectual resistance to decentralization. The roots of this resistance are examined more carefully in the next section. Here it will suffice to note the positive relationship between policy centralization and the infatuation in the 1960s with long-term "systems" models of complex society. It is no coincidence that works such as Jay W. Forrester's *Urban Dynamics* appeared shortly before Ottawa came to embrace the concept of federally initiated, hierarchical policy-making. Forrester's study, which is typical of the systems approach, first modelled the interrelationship among various activities in the city and then described how these activities changed over time as a consequence of various policy decisions made at the outset. Many readers will recall his most quotable conclusion, "that complex systems are counter-intuitive. That is, they give indications that suggest corrective action which will often be ineffective or even adverse in its results. Very often one finds that the policies that have been adopted for correcting a difficulty are actually intensifying it rather than producing a solution" (Forrester, 1969, p. 9).

If accepted, conclusions of this sort naturally compel one to argue for coordinated policymaking at the highest possible political level. However, aside entirely from the difficulty of establishing the parameters of a social-systems model and their change over time, the relevance of this conclusion both for policy and for policy-making is extremely limited. It can too easily create policy constipation by encouraging the view that no action can or should be taken until the whole system is known and modelled.

More than this, however, the Forrester-type conclusion suggests a naively one-dimensional view of policy evaluation – that the appropriate object of evaluation is the state of the urban system in some future, long-run equilibrium. But complex systems move complexly; the adverse results in Forrester's urban model generally appear only after the passage of many decades and may be totally overwhelmed by earlier and more directly beneficial results of policy, a point that emerges strongly from Jerome Rothenberg's (1974) review of

Forrester's urban model. The results of policy when applied to human societies cannot be judged on the same basis as one would judge the results of interfering with a mechanical system. Individuals are finely tuned to respond more to the pace and style of change through time than to the contemplation of a distant legacy. Since reaction to and evaluation of the path of urban change require local monitoring, and since both the reaction and the evaluation are critically important to the enactment of policy, centralization of policy-making demands extraordinary justification.

In order to deal at all adequately with urban problems we require a sophisticated understanding of the relationship among urban policy, planning and the activities of city-building, and of the way in which policy actually gets made and evaluated. This requirement constitutes the present urban challenge, and it is to a discussion of these matters that the next section is devoted.

Policy and Planning

The changing role that local governments have come to play in the years since the Second World War is the springboard from which any understanding of current urban policy-making must be launched. As Professor T.J. Plunkett has pointed out, before the 1940s, the municipal system "was not called upon to deal with issues involving conflicting values, difficult choices, or the development of any sense of community goals or objectives. Its role placed little emphasis on the matter of governing and considered its major purpose as a local public corporation designed to provide for the delivery of a relatively narrow range of community housekeeping services." Since then, "the role and scope of municipal government has been altered drastically and the decision-making process has not only become more complex but subject also to an infinite variety of pressures and demands. Municipal councils are now called upon to consider decisions that involve conflicting value choices as they confront more subjective issues which revolve around the currently popular concern for 'the quality of urban life'" (Plunkett, 1974, p. 617).

In considering these "conflicting value choices," humility is the first requirement. Only to those who never do it, is public decision-making a straightforward process of reaching for the right number and raising a hand in accordance with its dictates when the question is called. The surpassing inability we all share, to say on behalf of society what "ought" to be done, continually strains our unrelenting belief that some decisions are better than others. This constant tension might persuade us to abandon altogether the concept of a "better" decision but for an obstinate faith in the idea of deliberate, self-determined social progress. Because the reaction in today's cities against the destructive elements of out-of-control expressway planning and the inefficiencies of metropolitan sprawl has not so far produced a very sturdy set of alternatives, the process of urban policy-making as much as the policy itself has become of signal importance. Confusion over substantive policy is handled by diverting attention from the issues at hand and turning instead towards considerations of process.

But what institutions and which processes are satisfactory? This question, which takes us to the heart of the urban challenge, can be answered only by reference to basic concepts of society and social structure. Without some appropriate conceptual framework no serious discussion of urban policy-making can even begin.

In the public-finance literature it is possible to discern the outline of a standard model that might provide some guidance in this matter. Building upon well-worn classical concepts of economic man in individualistic society, this standard model begins by defining two separate roles for government. In the first of these roles, government acts simply to correct mistakes made by the private market; its role is to overcome problems of resource allocation. If the private market cannot provide appropriate amounts of parkland or roads or bus service or museum space, or if the market exploits the environment without paying adequate compensation or if it is unable to ration efficiently the production of exhaustible resources, then the government has a responsibility, according to the standard model, to adopt corrective policies. Its second and separable role is to redistribute economic resources among members of society in accordance with some general perception of fairness and equity. This role leads governments to adopt, for example, progressive income taxation schemes and various social security programs.

When applied to urban policies, this standard framework is

expanded to embrace several levels of government. The redistributive role is invariably assigned to upper-level jurisdictions – to the federal or provincial governments – while the allocative role is yielded to municipal government only for purposes of correcting market failures that exhaust themselves within the geographic territory of the urban area. If taken literally, this standard model of multi-jurisdiction policy-making would clearly rule out virtually any independent action on the part of municipal government, since someone outside any given municipal jurisdiction is always affected to some degree by decisions taken within the municipality. However, even when due allowance is made for real-life departures from the ideal situation envisaged in the model, the framework is still far too hide-bound for useful application to present urban policy problems. It lacks totally a sense of the process by which policy gets made, it offers no conceptual restraint to the complete centralization of every decision or policy matter that cannot be handled through the market, and its reliance on the assumption that allocation and distribution are separable government functions is especially difficult to maintain with respect to local-level spending.

Urban transportation spending, housing programs and the delivery of welfare services all have strong distributional implications.[3] Local governments have (weakly) taken the leadership in highlighting problems of distributional imbalances where the injustice is gravest – in the fields of housing, tenants' rights, physically handicapped individuals, single-parent families, and poverty in old age. From his examination of urban poverty, Professor Lithwick, in a companion study to his full report, reached the conclusion that "the vast majority of the urban poor...are not easily helped by simple cash transfers. They require a spectrum of tailor-made urban services..." (Lithwick, 1971, p. 65). While cash transfers and the progressive structure of income taxation are obviously our major interpersonal redistributional devices – and quite reasonably centralized to a considerable degree[4] – it would clearly be unwise to rule out a priori a redistributional role for local government with its high level of goods-and-services spending.

Our urgent need to break away from the standard model and the limitations with which it surrounds urban government is demonstrated by the increasingly aggressive interest local municipal councils are proclaiming in the social, economic, and physical well-being of the citizens they govern. In many cases this has resulted in radical personnel and political changes on these councils in the wake of recent elections. In our largest cities, reformism overtook the councils of both Vancouver and city of Toronto in December 1972 and it has been a strong threat in Montreal since the electoral success of the Montreal Citizens Movement in November 1974.

The significance of these dramatic political changes – in other cities as well as the big three: in Calgary, London, and St. John's – is that they have all emerged from and been built upon local concern over specific activities or projects. There is a constant processing of values and debating of day-to-day decisions at the local level that constitute the main ingredients of our emerging urban policies. Any conceptual model that is usefully to serve as a basis for new urban institutions and policy-making must be able to accommodate this local involvement.

The new policy bias observable in Toronto and Vancouver (among many other municipalities) in favour of public transit and against the private automobile, for example, was not created independently of the flow of urban activities in these cities. In both cases the seeds of subsequent policy are to be found in community assessment of specific projects proposed by authorities. In Vancouver, new attitudes towards city policies were early and strongly influenced by the 1967 debate over a highway interchange that was planned eventually to connect with a proposed Chinatown freeway; in Toronto, the climax during 1970-71 of a long-standing debate over the Spadina Expressway led directly to a clear articulation of reform urban policies. Elsewhere, the same phenomenon is evident: policies are developed in response to individual perceptions of specific activities. The reaction in Montreal to the destruction of low-income communities for expressways, to the demolition of Van Horne's house and to the proposed tearing down of blocks along Crescent Street has been escalated into a general position on urban development policy

Formally, urban policy may be thought of as a set of government instruments designed to influence day-to-day urban activities, with possible instruments ranging from an informal announcement by some responsible government official through to duly enacted council by-laws or acts of legislation by senior governments. This definition is straightforward enough, but it doesn't help us to understand where policy comes from or what might constitute good policy. Our understanding is advanced, however, by recognizing that major policy issues have been an integral part of the disputes that have arisen in cities over specific projects, that policy and project are inextricably linked in these debates.

What we have been witnessing, especially in our larger cities, is the gradual formation of explicit urban policies, the absence of which has so rightly been decried. Seventeen months after the cancellation of Toronto's Spadina Expressway in June 1971, Ontario had a completely new urban transportation policy which greatly increased the level of provincial subsidies for capital expenditures on public transit and provided for the development of both improved and experimental forms of transit vehicles; and in early 1974, the Council of Metropolitan Toronto, which for a decade had sponsored and bitterly fought for the Spadina, voted against building the Scarborough Expressway, another similarly situated, downtown-oriented road proposal.

Clearly there is an interaction between urban activities and urban policy-making that cannot be disregarded. While policy might indeed be influenced in various ways by circumstances and events quite apart from the activities it is directed towards, these activities are nonetheless the prime means by which the virtue of the policy is tested; and a judgement on the activities by the community will reflect back on the next round of policymaking. This signal role that public assessment of day-to-day activities plays in the formation of policy is contained in the often-expressed view that community groups or individuals in cities have a difficult time responding to broad issues of policy – such as the formation of a general urban plan or the creation of a national housing policy – but are able to participate fruitfully in discussions of specific projects. Without this activity or project monitoring at the local level, the evaluation of policy is virtually impossible. Bureaucracies, over-centralized and out-of-touch with reality at the activity level, are prone to what Harold Wilensky (1967, pp. 173 ff.) calls "information pathologies" whereby "intelligence fantasies" give rise to mere "illusions of reliable information."

Policy-making is not something that can be simply grafted, ill-fittingly, onto the standard model of fiscal federalism, something to be done as readily by bureaucrats in Ottawa reading journals about urban policy in foreign lands as by community groups in cities worried about their own local problems. From the process of policymaking that I have described, it follows not only that cities should be the prime source of Canada's urban policy but that they must be the single source of judgement.

Activating Local Government

If urban policy-making must arise from and be judged in accordance with local perceptions of urban activities, then some institutional means must be found of ensuring that the perceptions and the policies are linked. With the current upward drift of responsibility for urban matters, we lose in two ways. First, senior levels of government are deterred from dealing aggressively with urban matters by the continuing and increasingly noisy existence of local jurisdictions; and second, to the extent that policy-making is taking place at senior levels, it is hampered by ill-defined linkages with local communities.

If local government is to continue, municipalities – at least those with some appropriate minimum degree of political sophistication – must be assigned an independent and politically pre-eminent position in the formation of urban policy. At present our cities are inefficiently bound by the constraints of provincial legislation produced under a constitution in which local government has no specific role. While this provincial legislation is far from static, nonetheless many of its main provisions harken back to an earlier time when municipal government was less complex, perhaps less important, and certainly less desirous of being politically independent.

In the sensitive area of land-use control, cities are frequently forced to deploy inefficient instruments of policy through lack of adequate legislative freedom.[5] In each province, the basic structure of control is the same: zoning or restricted-area by-laws are the direct legal instruments through which the use of land is controlled. Master plans, taking on a variety of names, are generally expected to guide the zoning legislation and, in Alberta and Newfoundland, are by statute required as zoning guides (Rogers, 1973). For use in older cities now struggling with economic and social problems of second- and third-generation development, this current concept of a master plan seems quite antiquated, although all such formal plans are the recent products of post-war provincial legislation. The expectation that master plans will set out broad, long-term community goals to which subsequent municipal by-laws must adhere strains our collective community foresight to a degree not demanded of itself by any independent government anywhere in the world. In addition, since an official plan is not among the direct legal instruments by which a municipality affects its structure over time, lawyers and politicians especially have a tendency to want as inoffensive and innocuous a document as possible. As a result, master plans have tended to become inconsequential guides to policy, although they require in their making much busy work and through their deceptive pretence to policy relevancy may deter the urban planner or council member from striking directly to the heart of current policy needs.[6]

Policy-making in cities needs to be taken more seriously than master planning permits. It may be that we would be better served by separate policy statements in each of the several policy areas – land use, transportation, housing, welfare, open space, and so on. These policy statements, backed up by adequate research and public discussion, would then provide an appropriate foundation for various implementing by-laws. Perhaps through this device, we could displace the current planning preoccupation with relatively distant, terminal-year or end-state plans by at least an equal concern for the short-term implications of planning proposals. As the recent Graham Commission (Nova Scotia, 1975) has strongly urged, any such revised planning process must be closely related both to the urban capital budget and to forecasts of current budget revenue requirements.

While master plans may be ineffective or at best unwieldy instruments of urban policy, zoning by-laws can be extremely destructive of policy because zoning or restricted-area by-laws are the legally prescribed means by which municipalities establish direct legal control over land use and development, these instruments must often be deployed for purposes quite beyond their proper range of application. Zoning, as a legislative instrument, arose from the English common law concept of "nuisance;"[7] its application is to the external effects that certain uses of one lot might have on adjacent areas. Many of these external effects cannot easily be handled through a private market (often because of the many parties having an interest in any one transaction), so the ability to legislate constraints on use was established. Rogers (1973, p. 115) tells us that "the theory of zoning is that each district is an appropriate area for the location of certain uses which the plan designates, and that the existence or entrance of other uses will tend to impair the development and stability of the area for the appropriate use. The objective of zoning must be considered from the standpoint of the public welfare and of all the property within any particular use area."

Zoning, especially in large urban areas, must bear a much greater policy burden than this "theory of zoning" entails. Zoning is the major instrument municipalities have to guide their general geographic structure, yet, as I have shown elsewhere (Nowlan, 1975b), the short-term impact of a zoning change on the rate of growth of building space is quite unpredictable. Moreover, the zoning called for on the basis of local use effects may be in conflict with the zoning demanded by broader urban policy.

So far, provinces have either not responded to these difficulties or they have introduced some form of "development control." A succinct description of this instrument is provided in Alberta's recent proposal for a new Planning Act (Alberta, 1975): "The idea would be that some areas of a municipality are of such a nature that traditional zoning concepts are inappropriate...For such areas, councils would not have to list permitted uses or, for that matter, discretionary uses, but could, in a general way, indicate the type of development envisaged, leaving it to the administrators to deal with each application on its merits." According to Rogers (1973, pp. 137-8), "Newfoundland, Saskatchewan and Alberta are the only three provinces which have adopted a system of development control....Whenever a system of land-use control based on permits has been tried in other jurisdictions, the courts have firmly rejected its legality."

Because of the broad administrative discretion it gives to municipal officials, development control is clearly, and perhaps wisely, being approached with some caution. However, even this possible addition to the policy instruments available at the local level adheres too closely to traditional concepts of land-use control. It will be difficult to exercise these control powers in a discriminatory way: if one property owner is given permission to build at ten-times coverage one month, it will be hard not to give a similar applicant the next month the same approval even though two such developments might not be compatible with structural policy. In addition, this form of control continues to provide no way for municipalities to capture for public purposes some of the monetary benefits to be gained by more efficient city designs, a substantial portion of which will be capitalized in land values.

The whole relationship between beneficially efficient cities and internal city policy is in danger of being lost and forgotten as senior levels of government toy with the notion of constraining the size and distribution of cities[8] while leaving local government enwrapped in the cobwebs of old legislative restrictions. It is worth taking a moment to elaborate this point.

It's a fair presumption that cities exist because they are an efficient means of organizing the production of many of our physical and social needs. The dollar value of total output in a city exceeds the costs of production by an amount that might be called, for want of a better term, surplus value. In large part, this surplus value accrues to urban land owners in the form of higher land rent or land value than exists outside cities, although some part of the surplus undoubtedly is captured by other people whose services are at least temporarily in short supply.

Costs of production within a city consist of both private costs and social or public costs, where the latter are measured by the sum of official public expenditure and by environmental or congestion costs borne directly by residents. For any given city size and value of output, the level of private and social costs can be extremely sensitive to the city's internal organization. In other words, the distribution and density of land uses, the number and sizes of commercial centres, and the relative use of public transportation – all of which may be influenced by public policy – have signal effects on total production costs and therefore on total surplus value. For this reason, no useful meaning can be attached to questions about the best size and distribution of cities without reference to some particular internal organization. Our search for efficient city sizes should start not with fuzzy, ill-defined notions from senior levels of government about desirable inter-city distributions of population and economic activities: it should be based instead on the assignment of a clear mandate and appropriate policy instruments to urban governments so that within cities adequate attention can be paid to questions of organizational efficiency.

In the long run, that happy nirvana of the theoretical economist, land rents might reasonably be expected to reflect the true surplus value of urban economic activities, but in the sequence of short runs that constitute the real world, both the natural processes of change and deliberate internal reorganization will affect the distribution of well-being among urban residents. Individuals, restrained in their ability to move among and within cities, may come to benefit or to suffer unduly the effects of urban policy – unless municipalities are given policy instruments through which these short-run effects can be moderated.

Take a simple example. Suppose as a result of commercial expansion in the central area of a city, traffic congestion comes to impose inefficiently high social costs on both commuters and central area residents. Efficiency demands that these costs be shifted to businesses in the central area, but municipalities have no access to policy instruments that can directly accomplish this task. Ultimately, rising wages to commuters might produce some forward shifting of the costs, but even in the long run some portion could fall on owners of residential properties through declining land values. As a policy response to traffic congestion, the city might decide to widen roads or to develop more adequate public transit facilities into the central area. In either case, the cost of these changes will fall on taxpayers generally and not specifically on downtown business.

The inequities are not inevitable, but with the present inadequate set of policy instruments, they are unavoidable. Municipalities have no direct way of controlling the rate at which any given area develops, and they have no freedom to vary their mill rates according to location or use so as to recapture for the public purse some of the enhanced land value brought about through public spending; neither do they have legislative sanction for the introduction of novel fiscal devices such as an office-space sales tax which could be used in the circumstances of the above example both to deflect excessive central area growth and to pay for needed transportation improvements to serve the central area.

There is no need to spin out in finer detail the various specific issues that currently require resolution. At stake is the general fabric of urban policy, which must be based on some explicit concept of urban government. Our best course at the moment is surely to nurture the present political vitality of our larger urban areas, and to aim for more legislatively liberated cities.

David Nowlan is a Professor Emeritus of Economics and a member of the Graduate Faculty at the University of Toronto. He continues to teach and to do research and writing on urban and regional policy issues.

Notes

1. Based on calendar-year, National Accounts data. The best current source of urban financial information is the new 3-volume "Report of the Tri-Level Task Force on Public Finance" (1976).

2. The Tri-Level Task Force on Public Finance (1976) has calculated that, based on financial-management statistics, specific-purpose transfers from senior to local governments totalled $4,965 million in 1974 and $2,669 million in 1969. These transfers were 44 percent and 38 percent, respectively, of total local government revenue in those years.

3. Practice, in defiance of theory, has of course responded to these distributional implications. In the field of transportation, by way of example, the only published study of which I am aware that deals directly with the distributional implications of planned projects is a local-government study undertaken by Metro Toronto ("Metro Toronto Transportation Plan Review," 1975).

4. Transfer payments by the federal government to individuals and non-government institutions constitute about 64 percent of transfer payments by all levels of government.

5. This lack of freedom has two dimensions. The first, dealt with here, is the inability of municipalities either to create new policy instruments not already specified in provincial legislation or to drop inefficient old instruments demanded by law. The second is the right that provinces reserve to themselves and their agencies to review and revise duly enacted municipal by-laws. Makuch (1976) has shown the severity of this second type of constraint with respect to municipal land-use legislation in Ontario.

6. Within the context of planning in Toronto, these thoughts are further developed in Nowlan (1975a). From a national perspective, Rogers (1973, p. 38) comments that "because a community plan must be integrated legally, it inhibits the expression in such a plan of highly desirable statements of policy relating to

future planning goals." Back to Toronto, we find Professors Lang and Page concluding from their careful study of official plans within the Metropolitan Toronto federation that "much confusion pervades the presence of goal statements in planning – origins of goals is obscure...evaluation, to determine if selected ends and means were appropriate, is nowhere to be found in planning" (Lang and Page, 1973, p. 18).

7. Some history of zoning legislation is traced in Milner (1963). Mandelker (1971) provides a stimulating discussion of the need to rethink the present role of zoning. Mandelker notes that "use is the underlying legal concept on which the zoning ordinance is based" (p. 23).

8. For example, the latest (and unofficial) version of Ontario's Toronto Centred Region concept sets out with no analysis or rationale some preferred "mature state" populations for a number of cities and towns in the Hamilton-Toronto-Oshawa area (Ontario, 1975).

References

Alberta. 1974. Department of Municipal Affairs, *Towards a New Planning Act For Alberta.*

Forrester. Jay W. 1969. *Urban Dynamics* (Cambridge: The M.I.T. Press).

Lang, R.S. and Page, J.E. 1973. *Goals in Official Plans* (Toronto: Metropolitan Toronto Planning Board).

Lithwick, N.H. 1970. *Urban Canada: Problems and Prospects* (Ottawa: Central Mortgage and Housing Corporation).

Lithwick, N. H. 1971. "Urban Poverty," research monograph no. 1 in the *Urban Canada: Problems and Prospects* series (Ottawa: Central Mortgage and Housing Corporation).

Makuch, S.M. 1976. "Legal Authority and Land Use in Central Toronto," *Urban Forum*, Vol. 2, No. 3.

Mandelker, Daniel R. 1971, *The Zoning Dilemma* (Bobbs-Merrill Co.).

Milner, J.B. 1963. *Community Planning: A Casebook on Law and Administration* (Toronto: University of Toronto Press).

Metropolitan Toronto Transportation Plan Review. 1971. "Performance and Impact of the Alternatives Year 2000: Analysis of Income and Distribution Effects," Report 63.11 (Toronto: Metro Toronto Planning Department).

Nova Scotia. 1975. "Report of the Royal Commission on Education, Public Services and Provincial-Municipal Relations," Vol. II.

Nowlan, D.M. 1975a. "Planning Responsibilities in Metro Toronto: A Search for the New Consensus," in Bureau of Municipal Research and Social Planning Council, *Metro Toronto Under Review: What are the Issues?*

Nowlan. D.M. 1975b. "Development Control: Its Purpose and Economic Implications" (Toronto: City of Toronto Planning Board).

Ontario. 1975. *Central Ontario Lakeshore Urban Task Force Report* (Toronto:

Ontario Government Printer).

Plunkett, T.J. 1974. "The Implications for Decision-Making of the Dependence on Conditional Grants from Senior Governments and the Property Tax." 1973 Conference Proceedings, Canadian Tax Foundation.

Roger, Ian MacF. 1973. *Canadian Law of Planning and Zoning* (Toronto: The Carswell Company Limited).

Rothenberg, Jerome. 1974. "Problems in the Modelling of Urban Development: A Review Article on Urban Dynamics," *Journal of Urban Economics*, Vol. 1.

Statistics Canada. 1972. Advance Bulletin: 1971 Census of Canada, Cat. No. 92-755 (AP-4).

Statistics Canada. 1973. Special Bulletin: 1971 Census of Canada, Cat. No. 98-701 (SC-1).

Tri-Level Task Force on Public Finance. 1976. Report, 3 volumes.

Wilensky, Harold L. 1967. *Organizational Intelligence: Knowledge and Power in Government and Industry* (New York: Basic Books).